The
Emotional
L TWGcy

H **ting whole-school strategies**

Antidote

 David Fulton Publishers

in association with

antidote
campaign for
emotional literacy

For young people,
and all those who work in schools to help them realise their potential

David Fulton Publishers Ltd
The Chiswick Centre, 414 Chiswick High Road, London W4 5TF

www.fultonpublishers.co.uk

First published in Great Britain in 2003 by David Fulton Publishers

10 9 8 7 6 5 4 3 2

The right of the author to be identified as the author of this work has been asserted by him in accordance with the Copyright, Designs and Patents Act 1988.

David Fulton Publishers is a division of Granada Learning Limited, part of Granada plc.

British Library Cataloguing in Publication Data
A catalogue record for this book is available from the British Library.

ISBN 1 84312 060 7

Cartoon illustrations by Sam Smith
Typeset by Pantek Arts Ltd, Maidstone, Kent
Printed and bound in Great Britain

Contents

CONTENTS

Organisations are not simply products or buildings or cultures or traditions. They are all of these things, but fundamentally they are groups of human beings working together (more or less) to achieve often overlapping and sometimes shared goals. It is the management of their human needs, the release of their creativity, the coordination of their efforts and the creation of cooperative and effective communities which determine the productivity of organisations.

Michael West and Malcolm Patterson (1999)
Centre for Economic Performance, LSE

Emotional literacy is the practice of thinking individually and collectively about how emotions shape our actions, and of using emotional understanding to enrich our thinking.

Antidote's definition of
emotional literacy

Case studies

Introduction

Back in 1997 when Antidote held its first conference on emotional literacy, few were familiar with the term and even fewer recognised in it the seeds of an effective strategy for enabling schools to promote learning, community and well-being.

Six years on, the Department for Education and Skills is looking at how emotional literacy can be placed at the heart of our schools, and parents as well as managers and teachers want to know how schools can become more emotionally literate.

The book was written for all those who are looking to develop a strategy for embedding emotional literacy in the teaching and management processes of their primary school, secondary school or other educational organisation.

It is not a recipe book. Rather, it describes what an emotionally literate school might look like, and the ingredients that might go into making one. It recognises, though, that school members themselves need to determine how they will combine those ingredients to come up with a result that genuinely responds to the challenges they face and the opportunities that are available.

The first chapter, Emotional literacy basics, is designed to give readers a sense of how Antidote has learned to understand emotional literacy, what is involved in being an emotionally literate school and what the benefits are of striving to become one.

The next chapter, Elements, looks at what is happening when staff and students practise emotional literacy – taking an interest in what is happening for each other and using what they have learned to shape a more vibrant learning community.

Chapter 3, Contexts, is about how the different elements of school life can be shaped to foster emotional literacy. It makes the case that becoming more emotionally literate involves a school attending to the whole spectrum of its activities – specific practices focused on improving the quality of relationships, mainstream lessons teaching the curriculum, the processes that engage people in the management of their school.

Chapter 4, Strategies, explores how staff, students, parents and policy-makers can work together to embed emotional literacy in the fabric of school life, and makes the argument that it is through the cumulative efforts of everyone that an effective strategy can emerge.

Although most of what is described in the book focuses on ways of enabling young people to talk with each other, these activities need to be replicated also at staff and management levels. Teachers cannot create opportunities for others to practise emotional literacy unless they are enabled to do the same. We will give a fuller account of the sort of work that teachers, other staff and senior managers can do together in a future publication, *The Emotional Literacy Toolkit*.

The ideas in this book were distilled from conversations with so many head teachers, teachers, students, parents, researchers, advisers and others that it would be impossible to thank them all. They are the people who welcomed us into their schools, came to our conferences, took part in our projects or told us about their own, commented through our web site (www.antidote.org.uk), talked to us at events we attended, or answered our enquiries by phone and mail.

Special mention does, though, need to be made of the staff and students at Lister Community School in Plaistow, Gallions Primary School in Beckton and Avenue Primary School in Manor Park. As active and interested participants in Antidote's Emotional Literacy Initiative over the past two years, they have taught us much of what we now know about emotional literacy.

The main text for this book was written by Antidote's director James Park, and its case studies were discovered or commissioned by our researcher Alice Haddon. In many ways, though, the book is a collaborative document, whose creation drew on the insights and creativity of other Antidote team members: Harriet Goodman, Susie King and Anne Murray. Sam Smith drew the cartoons.

The writing of this book was made possible by a grant from the Calouste Gulbenkian Foundation. The thinking emerged through work in schools funded by the AIM Foundation, Bridge House Estates Charitable Trust, the Esmée Fairbairn Foundation, the JLD Trust, Lloyds TSB Charitable Trust, the Stone Ashdown Trust and the Tudor Trust. We thank them all.

Emotional literacy basics

The rationale for emotional literacy

Schools are complex organisations caught up in a whirlwind of different pressures. Teachers and other staff are called upon to tackle social problems, to deliver government targets and to satisfy parental expectations while holding firm to their core purpose – helping young people to learn and to develop their potential.

These pressures on schools can generate high levels of anxiety in staff and students. The effect of feeling pulled in conflicting directions, and driven towards goals that feel either unachievable or undesirable, may be a sense of discomfort that, over time, undermines well-being, generates disaffection and constricts learning.

Emotional literacy is a strategy for transforming this anxiety, and other difficult emotions, into productive energy.

Practising emotional literacy involves every member of the school community in thinking about how emotions shape their actions and in using emotional understanding to enrich their thinking. This increases individuals' capacity to access emotional states that will enable them to play a part in the evolution of a more harmonious and vibrant learning community.

Emotional literacy has a vital part to play in tackling what are seen as the three great challenges facing our schools today. This is because it can:

1 enable staff and students to find ways of feeling connected to each other, and of using their relationships to process the emotions that might otherwise cause them to lash out in rage or to withdraw in despair;
2 increase learning 'power' by giving staff and students the capacity to deal with the emotions that can render them unable to learn, and to access emotional states such as curiosity, resilience and joy that lead to a richer experience of learning;

3 help staff and students to engage in activities that promote both physical and emotional well-being, and to broaden the range of what they can talk about with each other in ways that make it less likely they will abuse drugs and alcohol, bully their peers or engage in other forms of self-destructive activity.

This book shows how schools can promote emotional literacy by paying attention to the quality of relationships within their communities, and by creating diverse opportunities for people to have the sort of conversations that will enable them to appreciate the thoughts and feelings of each other.

In an emotionally literate school, emotions still have the potential to disrupt the processes of teaching and learning. Staff and students will argue with each other, become angry, have negative thoughts and sometimes lose interest in teaching or learning. But when they do, the emotions that drive these situations can be acknowledged, talked about, dealt with and learned from.

Emotional literacy is not a strategy that can be confined to any area of the curriculum or indeed to any particular group in the school. It is most effective when it permeates what goes on in the staffroom, the classroom, the school's corridors and its playgrounds, as well as affecting how the school interacts with the wider community.

For emotional literacy to flourish, those who exert pressure on the school from outside – whether parents or policy-makers – need to be attentive to the emotional consequences of their own actions. This is more likely to happen when they seek to facilitate, guide and inspire rather than control and direct.

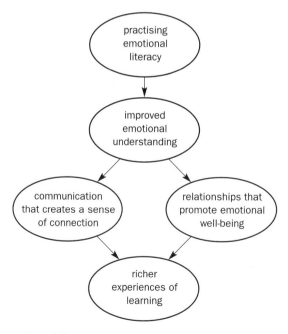

The benefits of emotional literacy

The ambitions of an emotionally literate school

In a school that seeks to foster emotional literacy:

Young people

- are given opportunities to explore the emotions they are experiencing in school;
- are engaged in actively building collaborative relationships with their peers;
- have people they can talk to when they are in distress or find themselves caught up in conflicts with others;
- are encouraged to be open with their teachers about how they experience lessons and other aspects of school life.

Teachers and other staff

- have a sense of shared responsibility for supporting, and learning from, each other;
- feel free to use their creativity in teaching their students;
- are encouraged to bringing their personal as well as their professional selves into the classroom;
- have opportunities to explore with colleagues any difficult and confusing experiences they have in their relationships with young people.

Parents

- are welcomed as participants in school life and the education of their children;
- are offered opportunities to share any problems they have in helping their children to learn and develop;
- can air and work to resolve any conflicts they have with the school.

Staff, parents and young people

- are valued for the whole of who they are rather than simply for the contributions they make to particular aspects of school life;
- are given reason to believe that they have a real role to play in shaping how the school is run.

By pursuing these ambitions, the school seeks to ensure that staff and students feel:

Safe – so that they can communicate what they think and feel to others;
Clear – about what they are thinking, feeling and doing;
Accepted – for who they are;
Included – as an integral and important part of the organisation;
Listened to – by people who are seriously interested in their feelings and ideas;
Competent – confident that they are doing well, learning, growing and able to achieve.

Four schools in search of emotional literacy

The four schools described below have gone some way down the road towards emotional literacy. They are not presented as models to be followed, but as examples to stimulate thinking about which elements of what they are doing might, or might not, be relevant to your own setting, and about how you might do something similar, but different, yourself.

Tuckswood Community First School

Tuckswood First sits in the centre of a working-class estate outside Norwich. The social and economic problems of the surrounding area suggest that this might be a difficult environment in which to give children their first experience of education (from reception to Year 3), yet the school buzzes with learning energy.

The source of this energy lies in the way Tuckswood focuses on encouraging children to be 'reflective, creative and critical thinkers'. This ambition runs like a thread through everything that happens in the school. In the classroom, the school council and elsewhere, children are encouraged to 'develop the ability to play an active role in their community and have a reasoned voice, being able to make a positive difference to the world they live in'.

What this means in practice is that every significant challenge that faces staff or students – intellectual, behavioural, social or emotional – can be turned into a set of questions to be actively explored with other members of the community.

Say, for example, a six-year-old boy has called someone names in the playground. His teacher might gather his fellow students to think together about the boundaries of reasonable behaviour, why people feel tempted to cross them and what they should do collectively to prevent people hurting each other. Out of this process a policy can emerge that the young people who devised it understand and want to see enforced. Nobody has been shamed or blamed, but a real commitment to better behaviour has been planted.

The same principle of encouraging children to say what they think and to work out their own solutions to problems is applied in lessons. One teacher, for example, followed a science lesson on the bi-hemispheric structure of the brain and the role of neurons by asking children to brainstorm their own questions. 'How did the neurons and dendrites get inside your head?' and 'Who made our brains?' were among the suggestions put forward. The question the children chose to focus on, 'Do neurons ever die?', led to a lively discussion of tentative answers and further questions. What they came up with would not necessarily win them points in one of the many public exams awaiting them, but there is no doubt they were engaging their brains in an active and exciting exploration of fundamental scientific issues.

At Tuckswood, children's capacity to work together on such deep and interesting questions is cultivated through weekly philosophy lessons in every classroom. Using an approach called **Philosophy for Children (P4C)**, children are encouraged to explore ideas, p.65 to ask questions about all areas of their lives inside and outside the school, to think, talk and really be listened to, away from curriculum pressures.

Through this questioning approach, the children address questions about what it means to live together and to work together. They explore each other's ideas, engage with the differences between them, learn how to help and support each other. 'Philosophy,' the school's web site says, 'teaches children to respect the ideas and opinions of others and to listen and build on those ideas, to be collaborative and to stand up for what they believe in.'

The same approach is used to address issues that come up between staff. When Sue Eagle took over as head teacher eight years ago, staff were feeling dangerously demoralised. She set aside time for them to discuss what motivated them in coming to work, and what would make their teaching feel more exciting. Out of this exploration they developed a statement of the values they wanted to promote in their work with children. Enthusiasm for learning, persistence in learning and curiosity in learning were the ones that came up alongside the importance of working with integrity.

Sue Eagle says that Tuckswood does not 'do emotional literacy' but that 'we are on the journey to becoming an emotionally literate organisation because of the way the curriculum is organised and the values we live by'. There is no curriculum time allocated specifically to learning about emotions, but this learning happens naturally during philosophy sessions and drama. The focus on questioning and collaboration means that emotions and relationships are continuously brought under the spotlight.

www.creative-corner.co.uk/schools/tuckswood

Buckingham Middle School

Many students who attend Buckingham Middle School at Shoreham-by-Sea in Sussex come from a local housing estate where relationships between families are sometimes fractious.

There was a time when these conflicts spilled out into the school. In trying to keep things under control, staff found themselves having to deal with some very challenging behaviour without being offered any strategy for improving the emotional and social environment. Feeling powerless to make things better – for themselves or their students – some staff even fell out with each other over issues of behaviour management.

Over the past five years, however, the school has steadily put in place a spectrum of activities within both the taught and the informal curriculum that are designed to get people talking to each other in ways that build supportive and reflective relationships. The intention is to evolve a warm environment throughout the school that will motivate teachers as well as students.

The starting point for the development of this process was a survey, which asked students to say something about their own experience of bullying in the school. How much of it was going on? What caused it? What should be done about it? All the policies that emerged were seen to flow from what young people had said to the interviewers.

Circle time was extended through the school to provide young people with opportunities to reflect on what was happening to them, to learn about each other, to air grievances and to explore better ways of working together. This was supported by a programme within PHSE lessons focused on helping young people to understand how emotions shaped their attitudes and behaviours. A **peer mediation scheme** was set up to help students resolve conflicts, and the **school council** was strengthened as a vehicle for giving young people an active voice in the school.

p.58

p.63

p.77

Buckingham's strategy for creating a more emotionally literate school has been so enthusiastically adopted by students that it has transferred into the local secondary school. Pupils arriving there from Buckingham insisted that they be provided with the same sort of opportunities for developing ways to understand, and work successfully with, each other as they experienced in middle school. The schools are now working together on developing awareness and promoting new strategies.

www.buckingham.w-sussex.sch.uk

Westborough High School

One half of Westborough High School's students are white and working class; the other half are Indian or Bangladeshi. The situation seems ripe for intense racial conflict. Indeed, some 20 years ago, mounted police were regularly called out to separate Westborough's students from those attending the nearby Catholic school.

It is very different now. As the school's prospectus declares, the school offers 'a very positive and relaxed atmosphere in which all students feel valued and cared for as individuals'. This is because Westborough's young people are continuously encouraged to talk through the difficult feelings they experience as a result of their encounters inside and outside the school. 'Westborough,' as recently retired head teacher Françoise Leake declared at an Antidote conference in May 2001, 'is a telling school. If there is a problem, it is talked about and dealt with. Things are never allowed to become issues.'

When students first arrive at school, they take part in an induction day which introduces them to the 'Westborough Way'. There they learn that discrimination is not tolerated, their prejudices will be challenged and they will be encouraged to find ways of working collaboratively with each other across their differences. They learn about the effects of bullying and racism, and the importance of respect for each other's cultures.

Throughout their school career, these messages are revisited in PSHE lessons and tutor groups. The aim is to ensure that students know each other and enjoy working together; that when they see one of their number having difficulties, they will support him or her; that if they experience aggression, they will have the confidence to challenge their persecutors.

Teachers are encouraged to make themselves available to listen to young people and to sort out any problems they may be having. It is recognised that students need many opportunities to explore their feelings and thoughts, to talk with each other about their problems and to find ways of dealing with them.

The Westborough Way is tough on intolerance and indifference. It recognises that students may sometimes have to be challenged to take each other seriously, but that there are enormous benefits for them as individuals as well as for the school when this happens. This can be seen in the school's academic record. Since 1992, the number of pupils achieving five GCSEs at grades A* to C rose from 8 per cent to a high of 39 per cent.

www.westborough.kirklees.sch.uk

Cotham School

Cotham School is an inner-city multiracial and multi-faith 11–18 school and Specialist Performing Arts College, with 1,250 students on roll. In its School Development Plan, Cotham makes an explicit commitment to emotional literacy.

It has set out a mission to 'raise standards still further through new ways of working' and has worked with all sections of its community to 'shape narratives that might help it work towards becoming in some sense an emotionally literate school community'. It is trying to find the stories that carry reason, meaning and depth to its work.

Its narratives are helping to build a distinctive ethos for its school community which declares that it wishes to 'place value on Courtesy, Honesty, Tolerance and Calm'.

What are the narratives that inform its practice and are they raising attainment still further? There are six narratives, each with a detailed script, which focus on:

- working with students about what it means to be learners;
- explaining the implications of being a multiracial, multi-faith community, and a positive guidance/holding environment in which young people can work and grow up;

- addressing issues of distressed or disaffected students through psychodynamic, therapeutic intervention; and acknowledging that behaviour is communication and difficult behaviours are often acting out of remembered hurt;
- asserting that the school will be successful if the staff, parent and student voices are heard, listened to and acted upon;
- working with feelings outside and beyond the curriculum seeking to be affective and effective rather than rational and instrumental;
- working with new ideas about leadership: design, building capacity, consultancy, seeing resistance as a resource for change, recognising the need to work with feelings of anxiety associated with loss and change.

As a school, Cotham has designed programmes that support and implement these key narratives. Its commitment to narratives and its focus on new ways of working are beginning to show in its academic results. Over a three-year period it will have raised its five A*to C grades from 60 per cent to 80 per cent, and shown an improvement at A2 performance from 14 to over 20 points.

www.cotham.bristol.sch.uk

Arguments for the sceptical

Some people reading this book will recognise their own practice in a lot of what is being described; others will feel that an emotionally literate school is something they can only dream about. Yet another group will feel some scepticism about the argument being presented, and in some cases this will represent a concern that what is being proposed will make their job more uncomfortable, complicated and demanding.

Below we try to address some of the arguments we commonly hear from teachers. In presenting our responses, we do not want to suggest that their points are invalid; only that we think there are ways round and through them.

1 There are enough emotions floating around my classroom without my stirring them up even more.

Emotional literacy is not about encouraging young people endlessly to pour out what they happen to be feeling. In many ways, it is the opposite of this. Emotions are part of being human. We feel them even when we cannot articulate what it is that we are feeling. Problems arise if we are always on the defensive against emotions being expressed. If, instead, we are given regular opportunities to explore and understand some of those feelings, we can reduce their power to create havoc.

2 It's this 'power to create havoc' that worries me. How can you convince me that emotional literacy is not a recipe for chaos?

There is clearly a risk that when people are given an outlet to talk about their distress, they will become overwhelmed by these feelings. That is why an emotional literacy strategy needs to develop gradually in response to people's readiness to engage with particular issues. It is not about suddenly pulling open the gate to feelings that have been completely bottled up until then. Rather, it is about creating a sense of safety so that people can start to share together what they are feeling. Then emotions will emerge in ways that are manageable both for those who are experiencing them and those who are on the receiving end.

3 But I am a teacher, not a therapist or counsellor. I am not employed to mop up tears from the classroom floor.

That is a useful distinction. There will always be people who need therapeutic help to process some of the more painful and difficult experiences they have had in their lives (see section on **therapeutic group work**). And while work on emotional literacy p.68 may complement more intensive work with troubled children, it certainly does not replace it. Our point is that *all* young people are helped to learn and grow if they are given opportunities to think about the feelings they are experiencing in the classroom. How are these affecting their capacity to listen, think and solve problems? What could they do at an emotional level to improve these capacities? What might other people do to help them deal with the feelings that are getting in the way of their learning? We argue that making it normal practice to address the emotional dynamic at work in the classroom, and in the school more generally, will benefit teachers, other staff and their students.

4 But nothing in my training prepared me to teach in this way.

It is true that some teacher training programmes pay less attention than they might to the emotional factors that stimulate young people's curiosity and motivation to learn, and clearly that needs to change. But most people have considerable common-sense understanding of what needs to happen in a classroom if they are to engage the emotions that enrich learning. They just need permission to act on what they know. If they are then given opportunities to pool their knowledge with other staff, and to reflect together on what is happening emotionally in their classroom, an emotional literacy strategy can begin to evolve almost spontaneously.

5 But surely the last thing teachers today need is to churn over all the negative stuff from their working lives?

Emotional literacy is a strategy for helping teachers to improve the quality of their working lives. It strengthens their capacity to take creative risks as they respond to the learning needs of students. At some point in the process, they may find themselves looking at the negative things they want to change. We try to ensure that, when they do this, they already have a strong sense that it is possible to improve them.

6 But isn't emotional literacy a bit of a diversion from our main task? There simply isn't time in the school week to do this sort of thing.

The first point to make about this is that emotional literacy is not necessarily an add-on to the existing curriculum. It is something you can practise within normal classroom teaching, as well as in other school activities. The second is that emotional literacy makes time available because it enables young people to take on more responsibility for their learning. They are likely to start working more effectively together and finding ways to stimulate each other. They are better placed to communicate information and develop ideas. Their teachers can spend more time sustaining enthusiasm, guiding students towards sources of information, reflecting with them on what they pick up and building their capacity to tackle the test hurdles they are going to confront along the way.

7 But does this not mean at some level challenging the government's concern about standards?

It is understandable why you might think so, given some of the things ministers say and do, but it still seems like a strange way of looking at it. Those responsible for drafting the National Curriculum were explicit about the importance of promoting 'pupils' self-esteem and emotional well-being' and of helping them 'to form worthwhile and satisfying relationships based on respect for themselves and for others'. They viewed personal development as underpinning academic achievement. The importance allocated to PSHE, Citizenship and the National Healthy Schools scheme were all seen as contributing to the accomplishment of these goals. The government is now putting even more emphasis on what their officials have chosen to call 'emotional and social competence', and on creating 'environments in schools that promote the well-being of teachers and students'. Although this interest has evolved out of a concern about street crime and young people's behaviour more generally, there is a growing recognition that it is important in other ways too.

8 Well, I think my teaching practice is quite emotionally literate, but you have to go with the grain of school life.

It is difficult for a teacher to be emotionally literate in a school where few other people are interested and there is little possibility of working on a strategy in a collective way. That is the real reason for the focus of this book on emotionally literate *schools*. We think that a truly effective emotional literacy strategy can only emerge when everyone – staff, students and ideally parents too, not to mention the wider community – has some sort of involvement in shaping it. It is the coming together of diverse people's efforts to practise emotional literacy, and the cumulative impact they have on each other as they seek to embed this way of operating into their daily activities, that makes this approach such a powerful tool for transforming school environments and boosting achievement.

9 But I just don't know where I would start.

We will be trying to help you find an answer to that question in the pages that follow, and addressing any further concerns you may have as they arise. First, though, here is a summary of the key points to come out of the discussion so far.

Emotional Literacy ...	
Potentially	*Is not inherently*
Empowers people to take initiative	About letting it all hang out
Challenges common assumptions	A new fad
Motivates the whole-school community	Disruptive
Transforms the school climate	Promoting a 'Me' culture
Enhances achievement	Against government policy

What is it about emotions?

Emotional literacy has an important part to play in enabling school staff and students to:

- access the emotional states that will support their learning;
- deploy emotional understanding to enrich their learning;
- foster the sort of relationships that energise their experience of learning.

Emotional states that support learning

Our ability to learn is clearly influenced by the emotional state we are in. If we are curious and engaged, we will take in information, pursue questions and overcome difficulties in the way of understanding. If, by contrast, we feel angry or anxious, it will be hard for us to take any interest in what is being taught. More than that, an ability to move between different emotional states helps us to carry out a sequence of different learning tasks. We need to be calm and open to absorb new data, intensely focused to analyse what it has to tell us and more free-floating to come up with intuitive and creative ideas about how to understand it. Emotional literacy is required to ensure we are truly effective learners.

Deploying emotional understanding to enrich teaching and learning

Emotions provide us with important information about ourselves, other people and the wider world. We learn from our own experiences of fear, shame, affection, love and other emotions how people are shaped by the needs they have of each other. The more we understand of what happens to us emotionally, the better we can appreciate the factors that drive relationships, shape communities and form societies. There is nothing about life as it is lived that we can understand without access to the information that emotions provide us.

Fostering the sort of relationships that energise the experience of learning

All learning happens through relationships. By sharing information with others and inviting them to provoke questions, reflect on our responses, evolve with us ways to think further about issues, we stimulate our capacity to think, and start to experience learning as an activity that is meaningful to us. It is only through our capacity to build relationships that we become fully engaged in learning.

Thinking and feeling

Given the evident importance of emotions to learning, one might ask why anyone would ever want to challenge the importance of emotional literacy. Nevertheless, the idea that we need to distance ourselves from emotions in order to avoid sloppy thinking is strongly held in our culture.

This idea that thinking and feeling are activities that can be distinguished from each other, commonly associated with the French philosopher René Descartes, has a certain common-sense appeal. We recognise that emotions have the power to affect our judgement and that emotionally based arguments can sway us to do things that are not in our best interests. However, to say that emotions can affect the quality of our thinking does not mean that they are not needed for good thinking.

In his book *Descartes' Error*, the American neuroscientist Antonio Damasio (1996) deploys a formidable array of neuroscientific research to argue that thinking and feeling should be seen as intertwined activities.

He illustrates his argument with the story of Phineas Gage, a building worker who, in 1848, was involved in an accident that drove an iron bar through his brain. Despite this horrific injury, Gage not only survived but appeared at first to be largely unaffected. Greeted as a walking, talking miracle, he could recognise objects, remember his past life and calculate much as he had always done.

He was, however, unable to formulate judgements, sustain relationships or direct his activities in a purposeful way. The result of the damage he had sustained to an area of his frontal lobe linked to emotional activity was that he became increasingly fitful and wilful.

Damasio's analysis is that you cannot think about anything important without having access to your emotions. When applied to education, the argument suggests that, if students are to solve a problem in physics, explain why Hitler invaded Russia or work out the most effective way to learn and get on with their colleagues, they need emotional literacy.

'Minds without emotions are not really minds at all,' says the neurobiologist Joseph LeDoux in *The Emotional Brain* (1998). 'They are souls on ice – cold, lifeless creatures, devoid of any desires, fears, sorrows, pains or pleasures.' The emotional and the cognitive areas of the brain rely upon each other. They drive our learning, inspire our capacity to remember and guide our judgements. They are, in short, vital to any intellectual activity that goes beyond the mere abstract processing of data. It follows that the challenge for our schools is to nurture the cognitive *with* the emotional, not against it.

How emotions affect us

Emotions provide us with the information we need to rapidly evaluate the situations in which we find ourselves and make decisions about how to respond. They tell us whether we should consider that a particular teacher wishes us well or ill; whether we should feel safe with our peers or scarper; whether what happens in the classroom has any relevance to the rest of our lives.

Contained in our emotional responses is all the information we have gleaned from our experience of similar situations. A teacher may bring to mind an adult who caused us serious pain. Being thrust into a group of contemporaries may evoke previous occasions when we experienced confusion and uncertainty. Each individual brings to the situations in which they find themselves a store of experiences that shapes the way they interpret other people's behaviour.

Clearly, therefore, it makes a great deal of difference what our past experiences of other people have been like. Have they made us feel safe enough to explore the world? Have they taught us how we can influence our surroundings? Have they helped us to develop ways of managing the emotions that the changing environment provokes in us?

Also important, though, is the quality of the experience we are offered in the current situation. Do we have the opportunity to discover that other people are attentive, respectful and responsive to our needs? If we are, we might be able to transform initial feelings of anxiety into a state of calm that enables us to reflect, converse and take in new information.

Consider, for example, the situation of a girl whose past experience might lead her to think that a boy in her class is threatening her. If left unaddressed, these feelings might cause her to become trapped in a condition of fear where she was unable to concentrate, learn or relax with others. But the presence of a kindly teacher who seemed to be interested in what his students were feeling could make her experience some safety. And if he could then facilitate her talking with the boy concerned about what was really going on for the two of them, she might find that he was not really a threat or that there was something they could do about it together.

Being encouraged to communicate positively with others can help us work towards states of calm well-being where we start to understand what we are feeling. We can take in feedback from others, allowing their smiles, grimaces, gestures and words to help us know ourselves, to distinguish our different emotional states, to reflect on how those states emerge from our experiences of situations. Out of these multiple experiences of human interaction, we develop the capacity to access, understand and respond appropriately to a wide range of emotional states in ourselves and in others. We become able to think both about what we are experiencing emotionally and about anything else that comes up. This generates the possibility of our thinking and feeling capacities working together.

Fractured links

When, by contrast, we find ourselves in situations where we not only experience sensations of insecurity, anxiety and stress, but have no one available to help us process them, the link between thinking and learning fall away. We become trapped with feelings that render us powerless and unprotected. There is no support available to help us tolerate and deal with this distress, nobody to make safe the experience of being in the world. The only way to endure such a condition is to disconnect our thinking from our feeling.

This strategy makes sense in the immediate conditions that provoke it, since it protects us from the unbearable nature of what is happening to us. It becomes problematic when it then becomes absorbed into our pattern of responding to certain sorts of situations, even when there is, in reality, a possibility of learning with other people. Then, instead of listening to what others are saying, thinking about what is being said and engaging with others in exploring the meaning of it all, we become overwhelmed by thought-stopping emotions.

One way of describing the situation would be to view thinking and feeling as two zones in the brain, connected by a bridge. When the bridge is well maintained, there is free traffic between these two areas of the brain. The information received in the emotional zone can be taken in, thought about, reflected upon, used to shape our responses and enrich our ideas. There is a possibility of interaction that is alive, buzzing and fruitful.

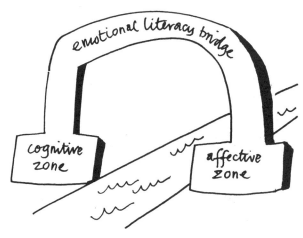

When the bridge holds

Picture the situation, by contrast, when the bridge has been neglected and started to collapse. It might be possible for some communication to take place, but it involves hopping tentatively across jagged fragments of the old bridge – the process is slow, dangerous and inconsistent. People lack the capacity to use the rich resources of intuition that their emotions provide or to think before they act. Their capacity to assess situations, formulate judgements and make good decisions is significantly impaired.

The more stress individuals have experienced or are experiencing in their current situation, the more likely they are to find themselves trapped on one side or other of the river, without the capacity to get across.

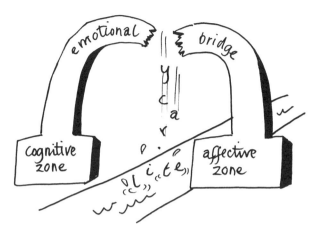

When the bridge breaks

Some may be impelled to cultivate a view of the world that seeks to isolate logic and reason from feeling – the model that Damasio argues against. This enables them to develop sophisticated capacities for shaping facts into arguments, but what emerges from this process will tend to be divorced from the reality of how other people experience the world. These are the sort of people who dream up products nobody wants to buy, design cities nobody wants to live in and write school policies that could never achieve their objectives.

Others, by contrast, may turn out to be completely dominated by their emotions. Whether angry, bored or excited, they seem incapable of being reached by reason. They act upon impulse and have little apparent ability to reflect on what they are doing or to think about how they might act differently. These are the people who disrupt meetings, try to get their way by bullying or manipulating people into submission and generally cause misery wherever they go.

While some people find themselves trapped in the affective zone, blocking off thought, and others in the cognitive zone, cut off from feeling, others swing from one side of the bridge to the other as the level of anxiety they experience starts to shift. An experience of being made to feel stupid in a staffroom, stressed out in the lead-up to an exam or frantic about an upcoming Ofsted inspection, may bring out the need to protect oneself from feelings that are experienced as dangerous or threatening.

Emotional literacy is about creating opportunities for staff and students to develop ways of moving freely across the bridge so that they can make full use of their emotions in teaching and learning. The relevance of this for teaching and learning is suggested by the table overleaf.

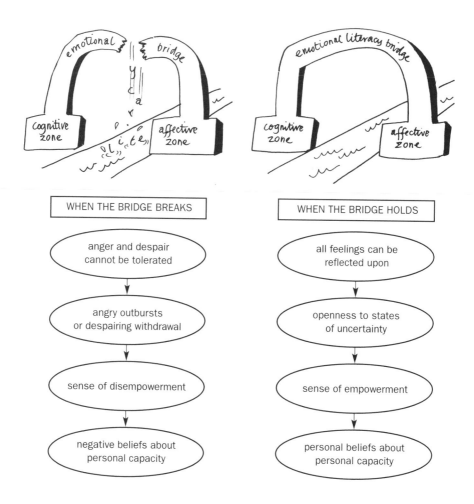

Emotional literacy helps to ensure that staff and students neither cut off from the information that emotions provide nor become so overpowered by emotions that they cannot think productively. As LeDoux has argued, 'We need to work towards a more harmonious integration of reason and passion in the brain, a development that will allow future humans to better know their true feelings and to use them more effectively in daily life.'

Evidence for the value of emotional understanding

The following research project, carried out at the University of Delaware, set out to evaluate emotional knowledge as a long-term predictor of both social behaviour and academic competence. The children who took part in the project were from economically disadvantaged families and largely African-American and European American. Some 72 children took part at the age of five and then again at the age of nine.

At age five, researchers assessed the children's verbal ability, temperament (according to the parents) and emotional knowledge. To assess emotional knowledge, the children were shown three pictures of facial expressions and asked to point to the one that they felt matched the researchers' verbal description. This recognition task made use of cross-culturally validated expressions of interest, joy, surprise, sadness, anger, disgust, contempt, shame and fear. At nine years, the teachers rated the children on social skills (assertion, cooperation, self-control, hyperactivity, internalising behaviour, externalising behaviour) and academic competence (skills in reading, skills in arithmetic and motivation to succeed academically).

The research team found that the emotional knowledge of the children at five contributed significantly to the prediction of behaviour problems, social skills and academic competence four years later. They found that emotional knowledge correlated positively with assertion and cooperation and that a lack of emotional knowledge correlated with hyperactivity and internalising behaviour (i.e. withdrawal). They found this to be the case even when temperament was accounted for, and suggested that failure to perceive emotional cues could seriously impede socio-emotional development. Also they found emotional knowledge to be a predictor of academic competence even when verbal ability was accounted for.

The reason for this, they suggest, is that lack of emotional knowledge may affect teacher-child rapport adversely, thereby decreasing the quantity and quality of educational exchanges and decreasing teacher expectation of academic achievement. In addition, a lack of emotional knowledge may lead to poor peer relations. This will affect morale, concentration and motivation to perform academically. They suggest that primary prevention programmes should begin early and include opportunities for participants to increase their skills of detecting and interpreting emotional signals and facial expressions.

Izard *et al.* (2001)

Useful reading

Damasio, A.R. (1996) *Descartes' Error: Emotion, Reason and the Human Brain*. London: Papermac.

D*escartes' Error* presents the scientific case for abolishing the division between mind and body. Drawing on his experience with brain-damaged patients, Damasio shows how a loss of contact with emotions breaks down rationality and argues that rational decisions require the support of our emotions.

Damasio, A.R. (2000) *The Feeling of What Happens: Body and Emotion in the Making of Consciousness*. London: William Heinemann.

The Feeling of What Happens seeks to describe the nature of consciousness and the biological source of our sense of self. Damasio's goal is to understand how we cross the 'threshold that separates being from knowing'; that is, how we not only know things about the world, via our senses, but how we are aware simultaneously of a self that is experiencing this 'feeling of what happens'.

Hobson, P. (2002) *Cradle of Thought*. London: Macmillan.

Drawing together work in psychology, psychiatry and psychoanalysis, Hobson looks at how thought emerges through relationships. 'If an infant were not involved with other people,' he argues, 'then she would not come to think.'

LeDoux, J. (1998) *The Emotional Brain: The Mysterious Underpinnings of Emotional Life*. London: Weidenfeld & Nicolson.

LeDoux describes how the brain detects and responds to emotionally arousing stimuli, how emotional learning occurs and emotional memories are formed, and how our conscious emotional feelings emerge from unconscious processes. He argues that there are many distinct neural systems, each of which gives rise to a particular emotion.

Emotional literacy and emotionally literate schools

What then can schools do to keep open the thinking-feeling bridge, to ensure that staff and students can use emotional understanding to enrich their thinking, and can think about how emotions shape their actions and behaviour? The short answer is that they need to maximise the opportunities for staff and students to reflect together on what is happening emotionally in their current teaching and learning relationships, and to build such opportunities into every aspect of school life.

Doing not being

Emotional literacy is an activity. It is not something you are but something you do. And it is something you do with other people. It is a way of managing your interactions with others so that you can build an understanding of your own emotions and those of others, then find a way of allowing this understanding to inform your actions.

Take a group of seven-year-olds, mostly rather lacking in self-confidence, who are about to face their first SATs. Each will have received a range of messages from their parents and teachers about these tests. As a result, some may have been led to the conclusion that the experience they are about to undergo will demonstrate their worthlessness and mark them down for a lifetime of failure.

One way that the school might respond to this situation would be to ignore the feelings being experienced. Exhorting the students instead to get on and do the work could appear to be a 'better' way of dealing with the anxiety. But the likely result would be that some of the young people concerned would be left with feelings of despair that rendered many of them unable to concentrate, focus or think about the subject in hand.

If the same group of young people were given opportunities to talk about their fears, they might find a way to move beyond them. Despite the way they had experienced parental and other pressures, they would be able to see the tests in perspective, to relax a little and to support each other in doing as well as they could. The chances are this would help to ensure they scored better in the tests, without allowing their experience of learning to be distorted by the pressure to pass them.

More social than individual

This example shows how people's capacity to understand what they are feeling is always as much social as individual. The same group of people will behave in a more emotionally aware way when they are given an opportunity to address their emotions collectively than if they are simply left to fend for themselves. And having learned to support each other, they are more likely to do the same when they face similar situations at a later date.

Emotional literacy involves using whatever relationships are available to help transform feelings that incapacitate into feelings that empower. The individual may well become better at using these resources, and will internalise some capacity as a result of this, but their level of emotional understanding is still influenced by the context in which they find themselves. We are always *in* relationships that powerfully influence how we feel and behave.

Someone who shows emotional sophistication while working with one group of people may be, to some extent, emotionally stupid while with another. What makes the difference are the opportunities that their organisation offers to address the pressures they are experiencing and the anxieties that arise from them. Emotionally literate organisations try to stimulate the sort of conversations and build the sort of relationships that enable people to understand their feelings and process any anxieties they may be experiencing.

They recognise too that you are not likely to increase your understanding of emotions if you are continuously trying to 'manage' them. If we are to use an understanding of emotions to enrich our learning and guide our behaviour, then we need to be open to whatever it is those emotions are telling us. Emotional literacy grows out of allowing apparently contradictory and perplexing emotions to bubble up and be thought about, not through trying to put corks back in bottles.

It is also not helpful to think of emotional understanding as a norm people need to be driven towards. Any organisation benefits from the fact that individuals have different ways of understanding and dealing with what is happening to them emotionally. Bringing their different perspectives into a dynamic relationship with each other stimulates discussion, debate and creative learning. Enabling these differences to be heard, understood and valued helps people to find more productive ways of being together and learning from each other.

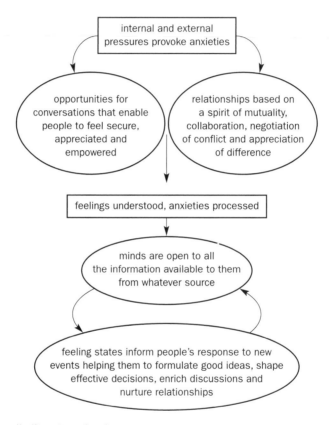

The emotionally literate school

Different ways of looking at emotional literacy

Helpful	Unhelpful
Located in the relationship between the individual and his or her context	Located in the individual
Something you do	Something you are
Is as likely to be developed through people's experience of relationships as it is through structured learning	Needs to be taught because it is unlikely to be caught
About being open to emotions	About controlling emotions
An ongoing process	About achieving set goals

I just want to ask ...

You seem to be inviting young people to engage in personal exploration. Surely that does not really belong in the classroom?

You are partly right. The focus of the exploration is not people's home lives or other personal experiences. We want them to talk about what is happening for them *now*, in this room and in this school. How is that affecting their capacity to learn? What could they do together to improve their capacity to learn? In the process, though, more personal feelings and experiences will come to the surface, and it does not make sense to block their expression.

Useful reading

Goleman, D. (1996) *Emotional Intelligence: Why it can matter more than IQ*. London: Bloomsbury.

In his best-selling book, Goleman argues that people may have a high IQ but not achieve well at work or at life. He points out that people who did well academically at school often failed to use their abilities when entering society at large. He draws on brain science to show how emotional processing is embedded in our neural circuitry, and argues for the distinctness of cognitive and emotional systems.

Steiner, C. and Perry, P. (1997) *Achieving Emotional Literacy*. London: Bloomsbury.

Steiner and Perry argue that emotional literacy is made up of three abilities: the ability to understand your emotions, the ability to listen to others and empathise with their emotions, and the ability to express emotions productively. To be emotionally literate is to be able to handle emotions in a way that improves your personal power and the quality of life around you. Emotional literacy involves being able to savour your own feelings, listen and respond to others' needs and fix emotional damage. The authors place significant emphasis on the importance of taking responsibility for the emotional mistakes that we make.

Reasons for taking emotional literacy seriously

The value of well-being

'Feel good, learn good' is the catchphrase that Peter Sharp, former principal educational psychologist in **Southampton**, uses to articulate the philosophy underpinning the emotional literacy strategy he helped initiate in the city. p.104

The phrase draws attention to the importance of emotional and physical well-being in ensuring that teachers and young people have the energy they need to learn and take an active interest in each other. An obvious caveat is that not all states of well-being are conducive to learning. Indeed, educators are charged with discouraging young people from seeking their well-being through drugs, alcohol, sex, retail therapy or aggressive picking on each other.

Being educated in an environment that encourages the practice of emotional literacy helps young people to distinguish between activities that will temporarily relieve emotional distress, and those that are more likely to assure lasting states of well-being.

Emotional literacy broadens the range of the conversations students have with each other. Through these conversations, they learn to find ways of transforming uncomfortable emotional states in ways that do not involve engaging in self-destructive behaviour. They can start to relax their guard with each other and to experience the sense of safety that enables them to acknowledge any self-deprecating assumptions they hold about themselves – I am stupid; I am ugly; nobody likes me – and to do so in ways that allow for the development of a more positive appreciation of their capacities.

Freed from pressure to win acceptance and affection by seeking to be 'the same' as others, no longer needing to 'pretend' to be someone else, they discover that they can be valued for who they are.

These conversations open up the possibility of richer and more satisfying experiences of relationships with others. When you know that there are people who value what you have to contribute, who will support you in making important decisions and negotiating the challenges you face, a sense of inner self-confidence and competence can begin to grow.

Within these relationships, people can discover ways to take control of their own lives and have a positive impact on the lives of others. They are put in touch with the diversity in their group, enabling them to enrich their own perspectives by engaging more fully with the world views of others. This frees them to discover their own reasons for engaging in learning.

Finally, the experience of emotional literacy – of opening up the connections between thinking and feeling – itself creates energy and well-being. It encourages people to stretch their emotional and cognitive faculties, to experience the excitement of generating creative ideas and to open themselves to a wide range of emotional experience.

I just want to ask ...

But I thought there was research that showed that getting people to talk about difficult experiences increased their stress levels.

Emotional literacy is not about forcing people to talk about things they are not ready to talk about. That would indeed be stressful. It is about trying to move away from the idea that you need to have a problem before talking about what you are feeling, and creating environments in which it is normal to address the way feelings may be getting in the way of learning and well-being, so that people feel comfortable doing that.

How we treat each other

Practising emotional literacy provides everyone in the school community – staff as well as students – with opportunities to manage the difficult emotions they are experiencing. It does so by providing them with structured opportunities to think about how emotions influence the way they behave, and to work out the principles that will guide their dealings with each other.

This builds on the recognition that young children are as capable as adults of thinking together about the way they treat each other. By doing so, they develop principles for guiding their behaviour that are different from those they might have imposed upon them only to the extent that they are more likely to be observed – because they have been developed by young people themselves.

Audrey Osler, who is professor of education at the University of Leicester as well as director of the Centre for Citizenship Studies, has written about a primary school in the West Midlands. Situated in an economically disadvantaged area where over 40 per cent of pupils are entitled to free school meals, the school has a system of **class councils**: pupils meet once a week with teachers to reflect on what p.77 is happening, to discuss issues of concern and to take decisions about activities for the following week. At the beginning of each year, the council draws up guidelines on behaviour.

These meetings are seen as a means of encouraging children to take responsibility, both individually and as a group, for their own *learning and behaviour*. They provide opportunities for discussing issues that concern them, and coming up with actions which address problems that have arisen. Osler concludes:

> This research, highlighted the valuable contribution which young people can play in developing effective systems of discipline in schools. Pupils made a strong link between being given opportunities for participation and the realisation of effective systems of behaviour management. Not only did the young people in this study express a strong wish to take a more active role in school, they showed a strong sense of responsibility and a willingness to contribute to the well-being of the school community.

An emotionally literate approach to behaviour seeks to help young people understand what provokes them, and others, to behave in the way that they do; encourages them to reflect together on what would make it possible for them to behave in different ways and seeks to help them process the emotions that trouble them. It also allows for the possibility that an individual's behaviour may be provoked by something in the way the school is run that needs addressing; or that someone may need some aspect of their current life situation – a bereavement or loss – to be collectively acknowledged.

At Antidote, we have often found that young people are perplexed by the behaviour systems operating in their classrooms. They might understand what they were meant to do in response to the various signals they were being given, and might be trying hard to do it, but this does not necessarily lead to them understanding why people want to manage them in this way. They attribute a lot of their 'messing around' to the anxieties generated by not knowing why teachers talked to them in the way that they did or why their peers behaved in the way that they did.

Emotional literacy seeks to create more harmonious interactions in schools by enabling people to understand the causes of their own behaviour and that of others. It seeks to avoid enforcing compliance in ways that restrict the energy which young people bring to learning or their openness to new knowledge. It sees bad behaviour as an opportunity to reflect on what has happened so as to stimulate further learning and to foster mutual understanding.

Emotional literacy encourages adults and young people to:

- own their own behaviour and recognise that they have an active role to play in defusing tension, negotiating conflict and improving the quality of the environment for everyone around;
- value themselves and their achievements in a way that makes it more likely that they will respect the contributions and achievements of others;
- empathise with others and see the classroom as well as the school as part of a whole system in which the actions of each member affects the experience of everyone else;
- collaborate and support each other in whatever they are trying to do;
- accurately read social situations and respond to them in ways that are more likely to result in satisfactory outcomes for everyone concerned.

Thanks to Jeanni Barlow for inspiring us to write this list.

Developing learning power

p.10 In the section **What is it about emotions?** we explored the extent to which learning is as much an emotional activity as it is an intellectual one. It was suggested that we can help to promote the quality of learning in our schools if we pay as much attention to the emotional dispositions that support young people's engagement with learning as we currently do the content of what is being taught.

At the University of Bristol, Ruth Deakin-Crick, Patricia Broadfoot and Guy Claxton have been trying to understand how particular sets of beliefs, values and attitudes come together to shape an individual's engagement with learning. They call this their 'learning power'.

Central to the seven 'dimensions of learning power' they have identified are learning relationships. Where learners isolate themselves from others, their engagement with the learning process is fragile. They cannot cope with significant challenges or the experience of failure. Where, by contrast, they have the self-confidence to work on their own and can also collaborate on the generation of collective ideas, they are more resilient, focused and able to make the best of every learning opportunity. The Bristol team argues:

> It is in the context of trust and affirming relationship that the learner can be challenged to take risks, explore, acknowledge uncertainty and confusions and develop self-awareness and resilience as ideas, concepts and feelings are reflected back and forth in the pedagogical relationship.

This finding highlights an important aspect of emotional literacy's significance for learning. Its practice involves teachers and other school staff in creating opportunities for young people to share, stimulate and support each other. They pay attention to the quality of the relationships between students so that they can be helped to have deeper experiences of learning. Case study 1 below demonstrates how this process can transform the climate in a classroom, and with it young people's ability to learn.

At the same time, the pursuit of emotional literacy provides opportunities for teachers to make themselves present to students in ways that foster a different quality of relationship, and profoundly impact upon young people's interest in learning. When, for example, the Gulbenkian Foundation evaluated a parenting programme developed by the Children's Society, they discovered that one consequence was its impact on some students' interest in learning (Hope and Sharland 1997). 'I look at her differently,' one student said of his maths teacher by way of explaining his improved results. 'Before, I didn't know she had any kids. Now I know that, we get on better.'

What about the other dimensions of learning power identified by the Bristol team – resilience, critical curiosity, making meaning, creativity, strategic awareness, growth orientation? What part does emotional literacy play in the capacity of students and their teachers to nurture these?

We have already suggested that, when people are working collaboratively together – drawing on each other for help and support – they are more likely to persevere in the face of difficulties and setbacks. Through our conversations with others, we learn to value the personal resources that we bring to different learning tasks, to draw upon the resources of others and to discover the pleasure of working towards specified goals. All of this helps us become more **resilient**.

We have also argued that when people do not need to defend themselves against unsettling emotions, their **curiosity** can be more fully engaged. They can take the risk of being challenged and temporarily unsettled by what they find out. They are able to tolerate what they do not know, to endure states of not-knowing so that new discoveries can be made. At the heart of emotional literacy is the practice of asking questions about what is really going on between particular groups of people. This process once begun, it can be extended out in ways that enable people to take a genuine interest in other topics.

What emotional literacy is seeking to engender in young people, and their teachers, is a condition of openness to information coming from any source. It encourages people to work through the ambivalences, uncertainties and confusions that come up as they allow emotional information to flow and be thought about. This requires a confidence that this information will make sense eventually, that there are links to be forged which will result in **meaning-making**.

What people are also developing through these processes is their capacity to work through the different emotional states provoked by the various learning tasks. They can be sometimes focused on carrying out defined projects, at other times in the sort of free-floating state that supports high levels of **creativity**. As Guy Claxton (1999) writes, 'Good thinking involves the disposition to think in different kinds of ways in different kinds of situations.'

Emotional literacy continuously draws the attention of those who practise it to how much they have to find out about themselves and each other, and what the conditions are in which knowledge can emerge. It communicates the reality that people cannot simply be divided into good learning sheep and poor learning goats. In this way it fosters **strategic awareness**, the understanding that learning is learnable, that we need to apply ourselves to learning if we want to learn.

Emotional literacy teaches us to move beyond fixed views of ourselves and simple generalisations about others. It opens us to the possibility that the next statement we are going to hear, or piece of information we are going to be given, will change some part of how we think or who we are. This flexibility and responsiveness is an inherent part of **growth orientation**.

In all these ways, emotional literacy is a necessary part of learning power.

I just want to ask ...

But is emotional literacy really compatible with the National Curriculum?

If emotions are integral to thinking and learning, then emotional literacy ensures young people are ready to absorb the knowledge and develop the skills laid down in the curriculum. It may be the case that there are purely cognitive ways of getting young people to the same place, and that these may feel safer because the outcomes are more predictable. However, they do not stimulate young people's desire, and capacity, to learn. That is why we argue that, ultimately, emotional literacy needs to be practised within the study of every curriculum subject.

You seemed to be suggesting that teachers should talk to students about their private lives. Is that really such a good idea?

That is not quite what we meant. We did give the example of a teacher whose revelation of the difficulties she was having with her children changed the nature of her relationship with one student. The point is not that teachers should discuss their family situation with young people. That would, in many cases, be wholly inappropriate. It is that teachers are more likely to engage the attention of their students if they can allow themselves to become known as people, whatever that means in particular cases. Practising emotional literacy helps in achieving that.

The seven dimensions of learning

Resilience

 Effective learners like a challenge and are willing to 'give it a go' even when the outcome and the way to proceed are uncertain. They accept that learning is sometimes hard for everyone and are not frightened of finding things difficult.

Strategic awareness

They know that learning itself is learnable. They believe that, through effort, their minds can get bigger and stronger, just as their bodies can.

Critical curiosity

They like to get below the surface of things and try to find out what is going on. They are less likely to accept what they are told uncritically, enjoy asking questions, and are more willing to reveal their questions and uncertainties in public.

Creativity

They like playing with ideas and taking different perspectives, even when they do not quite know where their trains of thought are leading. They are more receptive to hunches and inklings that bubble up into their minds, and make more use of imagination in their learning. They understand that learning often needs playfulness as well as purposeful, systematic thinking.

Making meaning

They are on the look-out for links between what they are learning and what they already know. They get pleasure from seeing how things 'fit together'. They like it when they can make sense of new things in terms of their own experience, and when they can see how learning relates to their own concerns.

Growth orientation

They are interested in becoming more knowledgeable and more aware of themselves as learners. They like trying out different approaches to learning to see what happens. They are more reflective and better at self-evaluation. They are more able to talk about learning and about themselves as learners. They know how to repair their own emotional mood when they get frustrated or disappointed. They like being given responsibility for planning and organising their own learning.

Learning relationships

They are good at managing the balance between being sociable and being private in their learning. They like to learn with and from others, and to share their difficulties when it is appropriate. They acknowledge that there are important other people in their lives who help them learn. They make use of others as resources, as partners and as sources of emotional support.

These dimensions have emerged from the ELLI (Effective Lifelong Learning Inventory) project led by Ruth Deakin-Crick, Patricia Broadfoot and Guy Claxton.

Case study 1

Teenagers discover different ways of behaving and learning together through dialogue about what is happening emotionally in the classroom

This class of Year 9 students from an inner-London mixed comprehensive had a reputation for being exhausting and unmanageable. The specific behaviours that teachers complained of were their seeming inability to even want to listen to the teacher, or each other for that matter, and the way the girls who made up half the class had evolved a passive stance which was clearly impeding their achievement in many areas. Teachers complained that it was not possible to engage with the students in a meaningful way. This left them with a range of feelings from frustration to anger. In the case of one teacher, relations had almost completely broken down.

p.25

Antidote began by administering the ELLI (Effective Lifelong Learning Inventory) tool for assessing students' **learning power**, developed by Ruth Deakin-Crick at the University of Bristol. Analysis of the results proved that the class was composed of reasonably effective learners. This came as a surprise to both the tutor and the Head of Year. Deakin-Crick suggested that the school might work with the class members particularly on their strategic awareness and meaning-making.

We could have decided to do some work around listening skills, but we felt that getting students to explore together what might be preventing them from being able to listen would probably be more productive. It is often assumed that students who do not listen lack the required skills. In reality, they may have the skills but choose not to apply them because of something that is happening in the whole situation. Our hunch was that, if we could offer the students and teachers a framework for coming together to think about what the emotional experience of being a student in this form might be, the reasons for their inability to listen might become clearer to all.

We felt from all that we knew about the role of the emotions in learning that the level of difficulty the students had with listening to, and engaging with, their teachers and each other could be thought about as a communication which carried valuable information about the students' experience of the class, and how this might be impacting on their learning. Our hypothesis was that, if we tried to pay attention to what the students might be communicating through these behaviours, then perhaps we could devise ways of addressing the underlying issues. We felt we would be helped in this by creating an opportunity for students and their teachers to explore possible meanings together.

This resulted in a day at the end of the autumn term when all the students, their Head of Year, their tutor, two of their subject teachers and two consultants from Antidote went out of school to a local community learning venue to spend time together exploring the emotional experience of being a student in their class.

We spent the morning using a drama exercise where the students had to imagine themselves as a group of strangers who had survived a plane crash in the rainforest. Beforehand we told them that they would earn points for certain qualities of teamwork which we defined for them. The teachers observed and were responsible for awarding points when they saw evidence of the students using teamwork skills. Basically the drama used metaphor to represent the kinds of social and emotional situations that the students faced on a daily basis as a group in school.

In the afternoon the students and teachers began to make the links between the metaphorical drama and the real life of the class, in particular the difficulties they had working as a team and including all their peers respectfully in the task of learning. The issue of gender difference and the mutual suspicion and distrust across the genders was the main 'hot topic' that the students wanted to talk about.

At the end of the day, the students felt a certain relief at just having been able to talk about what was on their minds. The teachers, by contrast, expressed frustration that we had not managed to set targets with the students for next term. It was not possible to resolve this highly charged emotional issue in the time we had available.

In the first drama lesson after this session, the teacher and the Antidote consultant reminded the students that it was the gender issue that they had said they wanted to work on. We said we did not have any answers, but that the drama teacher would work with them for as long as it would take to help them achieve progress on this. The English teacher also picked up on a number of other aspects of their relationships that had arisen on the day.

Over the following term, both teachers were delighted at the learning progress being made by the class. Each found themselves starting to look forward to working with them. They were no longer having difficulties being attended to or listened to, and the girls were making great progress in claiming their voice in both lessons. The form tutor reported that they seemed to have matured since the beginning of the year.

We believe it was extremely significant that the students were able to openly express their concerns to each other in the presence of their teachers. Interestingly, the teachers were more anxious about finding a solution (as expressed in their desire to set targets) than the students. It was perhaps being given an opportunity to be listened to by their teachers that enabled the students to feel they could listen to their teachers in turn.

We had provided teachers with a safe opportunity to listen to students who were 'stuck' in negative social and emotional dynamics in the here and now of their schooling. By acknowledging the issues without having a solution or target in mind, the message was given to the students that their teachers could hear what they were saying and stay with it even when it was difficult to know what to do. They could trust that the students would be able, over time, to resolve the issue for themselves, albeit with continued support from the teachers. This experience modelled for students the importance of paying attention to each other and to what was going on at the interpersonal level. As one of the teachers said, 'They felt we cared enough about them to do this with them.'

Anne Murray (Antidote)

Useful reading

Claxton, G. (1999) *Wise Up: The Challenge of Lifelong Learning*. London: Bloomsbury.

Wise Up uses new sciences of brain and mind to reveal that everyone has the capacity to become a powerful, lifelong learner if they only learn how to learn. It shows how to encourage resilience and resourcefulness in young people.

Claxton, G. (2003) *Building Learning Power*. Bristol: TLO.

Building Learning Power takes some of the research carried out by Claxton and his colleagues at the University of Bristol, and turns it into a practical guide for teachers seeking to cultivate good learning in their pupils.

Dweck, C.S. (1999) *Self Theories: Their Role in Motivation, Personality and Development*. Philadelphia, PA: Psychological Press.

Dweck believes that children fall into two broad groups. In the first (entity theory) group, they believe that the factors determining behaviour and intelligence dwell within us and are unlikely to change. In the second (incremental theory) group, intelligence and behaviour are not fixed but can be cultivated and are open to change. Their behaviour, intelligence and social roles are determined by which of these groups they belong to.

Greenhalgh, P. (1994) *Emotional Growth and Learning*. London: Routledge.

Greenhalgh argues that learning depends on security in one's identity. Our capacity to learn requires an ability to manage our inner and outer worlds. If we are unable to manage our emotions, we are likely to lose our capacity for imagination. We become frozen and emotionally stuck, unavailable for learning. Emotional growth is necessary for learning to take place.

Salzberger-Wittenberg, I., Williams, G. and Osborne, E. (1983) *The Emotional Experience of Teaching and Learning*. London: Routledge.

This pioneering book looks at the kind of experiences that enable the growing child to attain his or her potential and the emotional factors that can facilitate or hinder learning. Tracing the complex relationship between academic achievement and personal growth, it demonstrates how significant is the quality of relationships.

2

Elements

This chapter describes the five activities that young people and their teachers need to engage in if they are to foster an emotionally literate environment:

1 developing a language to put into words the feelings they are having;
2 finding a space to discover their own feelings, and how these are shaped by the situations in which they find themselves;
3 asking questions of other people about what they are feeling, so that they can compare different experiences to their own;
4 engaging in dialogue with each other about their thoughts and feelings;
5 shaping out of everything they have learned about themselves a personal narrative that enables them to experience their life as meaningful and valuable.

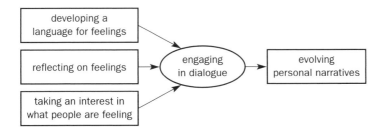

Developing a language for feelings

If staff and students are to explore together what is happening for them in their lives at school, they need to develop a language that can capture the nuances of emotional experience and help them navigate the grey areas between 'happy' and 'sad', 'angry' and 'calm', 'confident' and 'ashamed'.

Our ability to expand the language we use for speaking about emotions grows through practice. Such practice becomes an everyday part of school life when staff and students:

- feel they have permission to explore feelings;
- sense that it will be safe for them to do so;
- are offered explicit opportunities for such conversations.

Permission to speak

Young people can easily pick up that they do not have permission to speak about their feelings in school. They have been separated from their more-or-less nurturing homes, thrust into a large group of their peers, then told that they must start to develop new skills and engage in the busyness of school life. It is hardly surprising if some become wary, and reply to questions about what they are feeling with an unrevealing 'Okay' or 'I don't know'.

School staff will counter this if they communicate actively that they *are* interested in young people's feelings. At Mason Moor Primary School in **Southampton** p.104 this message is made crystal clear. Throughout the school year, staff and students explore together a range of different feelings. Posters go up on corridor walls and displays are laid out in the library. Teachers build the exploration of these feelings into their lessons and encourage children to draw pictures, write poems and create their own presentations on a range of contrasted emotions – angry/calm, sad/happy, intimidated/confident, ashamed/proud, lonely/sociable. The intention, according to former head Sue Nicholson, is to give young people 'a vocabulary to express their feelings so that they have a range of words to draw on and apply in their writing'.

Finding safety

People need different sorts of reassurance to engage in conversations about emotions. Some may need convincing that whoever is supervising the process really will maintain whatever ground rules have been established. Some may need someone to reassure them that they will not be compelled to divulge things they are not ready to share, or to venture into areas that challenge their cultural, religious or familial taboos. Others may want to be absolutely sure that nobody will use this information against them.

The reason for this sensitivity is that any conversation about emotions can bring people into contact with areas where they feel personally vulnerable. One cannot talk intelligently about feelings without at some level connecting to one's own experience. Despite this, people are likely to feel safer if the conversation at least starts on ground that is not personal.

There are many ways of drawing people into the exploration of fictional situations. Inviting young people to work out what is going on emotionally as they play with puppets, act out imaginary situations or talk about stories they have read together draws them towards their own emotional experience. They can compare the story they are exploring against their own. They may identify with particular feelings in the characters and recall times when they felt the same way. Even when we are not conscious of it, the process of understanding our own emotions becomes woven into the process of understanding other people's.

The strength of students' reluctance to talk about themselves directly, as opposed to their enthusiasm for doing so indirectly, was suggested in an exercise carried out by Eric Hall and Andrew Kirkland (1984) from the University of Nottingham. They invited a group of young adolescents to spend 20 minutes writing about the experience of their school holidays, and another 20 minutes writing about the life of a tree. The difference in the level of emotional statements between the two accounts was striking – some 12 per cent about the holidays contained emotional statements as against 57 per cent of statements about the tree. There was a striking predominance in the tree accounts of those emotions – sadness, anger and hurt – that can be difficult to acknowledge to a group of peers.

The way in which young people move between thinking about themselves and thinking about others illustrates that this approach is about more than simply getting them to the point of being able to talk freely about their feelings. Emotional literacy requires us to understand others and ourselves through the dynamic interplay of our different experiences. It is about finding a third position slightly outside ourselves, distanced from the intensity of our current emotional experience, where we can see what is happening to us and reflect upon it. Emotional literacy is about having enough emotional cool to appreciate what is getting us so heated or leaving us so down.

Creating opportunities

Every activity described in this book involves setting up group situations where people can explore experience through the eyes of others and, in the process, start finding ways to be more open about themselves and to learn about others. The two case studies below illustrate the way this can work.

Case study 2 shows how two six-year-old boys were provoked by a story about a stick insect, Zippy, to talk about their own experiences of bereavement. The teacher picked up on one boy's account of his loss and, by sensitively exploring it with his fellow students, enabled another more troubled boy to talk about his own painful experience. Moments of revelation such as this that have the potential to transform the way individuals relate to their teachers and their peers.

Case study 3 concerns a project in Sheffield which used drama and **circle time** p.58 in a way that helped young people enlarge their emotional vocabularies. The work transformed their ways of being with each other, and also engaged them in an experience that was inherently joyful.

Helpful and unhelpful ways of viewing emotions

Helpful	Unhelpful
Feeling anger, jealousy and hate is a natural part of life	We are bad people if we have 'negative' feelings
It is possible to transform distressing emotions into more positive states	There are some emotions it would be better not to experience
Feelings emerge through the interaction between ourselves and others	Other people make us feel the way we do
We can learn different ways of responding to situations	Particular sorts of situation will always generate the same feelings in us

Thanks to Lynne Gerlach and Julia Bird of Sowelu Associates for inspiring the ideas in this table.

Case study 2
How a stick insect gets six-year-olds talking about their feelings

 Zippy's Friends is a school-based programme developed for six-year-olds. It teaches children how to cope with everyday difficulties, to identify and talk about their feelings and to explore ways of dealing with them. It also encourages them to help each other deal with problems.

The programme is built around a set of six stories. Zippy is a stick insect and his friends are a group of young children. The stories show them confronting issues that are familiar to young children, such as friendship, communication, feeling lonely, bullying, dealing with loss and making a new start.

Zippy's Friends encourages children to explore and think for themselves. It demonstrates the importance of talking to other people when we feel sad or angry, and of listening to other people when they feel sad or angry. It affirms a child's ability to both use and give support.

One teacher told a remarkable story about the session that deals with death and dying. A seven-year-old called Alexander told the class that his sister Camilla had died a year ago. He explained exactly what had happened and where she was buried. The teacher asked Alexander whether he would like all the children to go to the graveyard where Camilla was buried. He said he would and so they went together. Each child took a flower to put on Camilla's grave, and they had lots of questions for Alexander and the teachers. They were practical questions such as 'Where is Camilla?' 'Which way is she lying?' and 'Where are her feet?'

One blond boy, who was often very disruptive, quietened down a lot during this discussion. When the children returned to the classroom, he surprised everyone by saying: 'When I get to the graveyard, I kneel down on the ground and I feel that I can talk to my grandparents.' The teacher was delighted that the class joker had felt able to share his feelings in this way.

When asked how the programme has changed their children, teachers often report that they have become much better at resolving conflicts. One boy in a Danish school replied to a question about what he had learned from the programme: 'I know what to do now when somebody thumps me. I don't thump him back. I ask him why he's doing it.'

There have been two evaluations of the programme. The first showed that there had not been sufficient improvement in children's coping skills, which led to a comprehensive review of the materials. A follow-up evaluation found that children in the programme showed clear improvements in their abilities to cope with everyday problems, compared to those in control groups. They also improved in cooperation, empathy, self-assertion and control.

Chris Bale (Partnership for Children)

Case study 3

A whole-school approach to giving young people a language in which to talk about their emotions

The Taking Care Project was a whole-school approach to emotional literacy implemented by three primary schools in a socio-economically deprived area of Sheffield.

p.55

Its aim was to address the social, emotional and educational aspects of children's well-being through the delivery of **circle time**, drama and whole-school well-being meetings. Very high numbers of children at these schools were living in situations of adversity that affected their ability to understand and handle feelings; for example, research-based estimates suggest that between two and four children in a class of 30 would be living in a home where domestic violence was an issue.

Each of the three schools nominated a particular year group to take part in the programme. The community psychologist ran five half-day experiential training workshops for teachers, support teachers and school nurses from the participating schools. These were designed to equip them to deliver a programme of ten Taking Care sessions in each school.

For ten weeks, each class worked through a programme that roughly followed the same sequence, covering self-respect, relationships, feelings, bullying, violence and available networks of support.

Evaluation of this project involved children being interviewed before and after the sessions, using scenarios of bullying and domestic conflict to elicit feelings, words and help-seeking intentions. Teachers were asked to rate individual children and the whole class before and after the sessions. Facilitators and head teachers were interviewed on the impact of the sessions.

The evaluation showed that sessions were beneficial to nearly all the children involved. There were significant improvements across both age and gender in the ability to express emotions and to seek help from others. The younger children significantly increased the number of feelings words they used spontaneously. They were using words such as miserable, glad, surprised and jealous, as opposed to the simpler words such as sad and happy used before the sessions. Even for the nine-year-olds, where the effect was less marked, the range of words increased to include words such as grateful and lonely.

Children showed an increase in the number of people from whom they intended to seek help. Boys showed more significant benefits than girls in emotional expression and help-seeking intentions, but teachers rated the girls as showing more improvement in classroom behaviour. The most significant changes that teachers identified were an increased confidence in work and a reduction in disruptiveness.

The majority of the children had enjoyed the sessions and wanted them to continue. They had a clear idea of what the sessions were for, and had appreciated the way drama activities enabled them to express their own experiences and feelings. Head teachers valued the whole-school well-being meetings as they led to increased multi-agency co-ordinated support and new collaborative initiatives in each school.

Heather Hunt and Gill Crow (2001)
Heather.Hunt@care4free.net

I just want to ask ...

But where is the dividing line between talking about personal issues and talking about the emotional issues that might affect people's ability to learn?

The dividing line is not drawn around *what* people are talking about, but around *why* they are doing so. We want people to talk about their feelings in the classroom so that they can trust each other, work collaboratively together and use emotional knowledge in their learning. Keeping that purpose in mind shapes the way these feelings emerge in discussion and how they are then dealt with.

Surely feelings do not have to be articulated to be felt and understood?

You are right to suggest that a lot of emotional understanding evolves without words and that we communicate in many non-verbal ways. Ultimately, though, language is a part of how we construct meaning out of our experience. For understanding really to grow between groups of people, some things do need to find their way into words.

Useful resources

Primary

Equal Voice, Pop-Up Theatre.

A video and book containing a set of techniques and games designed to create a safe space for looking at fictional conflicts between people and to enable the development of emotional expression. The work is designed to improve young people's ability to be emotionally articulate by creating an atmosphere of trust that allows children to experiment with alternative ways of behaving. See Appendix 1 for details.

Rae, T. (1998) *Dealing with Feeling – An Emotional Literacy Curriculum.* Bristol: Lucky Duck Publishing.

This book covers a range of different emotions – angry, sad, happy, surprised, loved, shocked, bored, jealous, ashamed, lonely, greedy, nervous, disappointed, rejected, shy, arrogant, generous, selfish and intimidated. After introducing each emotion, the book provides a narrative account of situations that might engender such a feeling, suggests ways of discussing and role-playing to experience the emotions in safety and learn to empathise with others. Used by Mason Moor Primary School in Southampton to develop the approach described above.

Webster-Stratton, C. (1999) *How to Promote Children's Social and Emotional Competence.* London: Paul Chapman Publishing.

Shows how teachers can work with parents to address the educational and emotional needs of children from four to eight years. Includes games, activities and strategies for the classroom.

Zippy's Friends (case study 2): available from Partnership for Children. See Appendix 1 for contact details.

Primary and Secondary

Bristol City Council, *The Emotional Literacy Hour: Working Towards Emotional Literacy.* Bristol: Lucky Duck Publishing.

This video shows a group of primary and secondary schools in Bristol working with pupils on their emotional literacy through approaches such as assemblies, drama role-play, puppets, circle time and group discussions.

Secondary and beyond

Brearley, M. (2001) *Emotional Intelligence in the Classroom: Creative Learning Strategies for 11–18s.* Bancyfelin: Crown House Publishing.

This book summarises current research on emotional intelligence and learning, and offers practical strategies for use with secondary students.

Getting Connected, Young Adult Learning Partnership (NIACE) (see Appendix 1 and www. gettingconnected.org.uk).

Described as a curriculum framework for social inclusion, these materials are designed to help disengaged and disillusioned young adults (16–25) to reconnect with learning and activities likely to foster their personal development so as to develop the 'soft' skills involved in managing their lives and relationships. Its six modules are: Knowing myself; Connecting with feelings; Holding beliefs; Handling relationships; Getting and giving support; Exploring risks. The first evaluation of this programme suggested that there was a positive impact on young people in terms of their self-awareness, self-management, motivation and ability to manage relationships, as well as their social inclusion.

Making a Connection, contact Children and Youth Partnership Foundation (see Appendix 1).

Curriculum materials for students at KS3 seeking to acquire and practise life skills which will help them understand their own personal resources and social interactions. Covers emotional literacy alongside thinking skills, creative conflict resolution and active citizenship. Organised into three modules entitled: Connecting with yourself; Connecting with others; and Connecting with the community.

See Appendices 1 and 12 for organisations offering processes for developing emotional language.

Reflecting on feelings

Schools are often frenzied places. Students and staff rush between their lessons and apply themselves to a range of different tasks. Someone once said that the words heard most often by today's children and young people are 'hurry up'. The message is that time is short and they must get on.

This pressure can cause stressful emotions to build up through the school day. A sense of collective tension may come from an accumulated sequence of events – a student losing his temper, a confrontation in the playground, the uncomfortable ritual of queuing for lunch. It may be compounded by something that is happening in the wider world – a brutal child murder that leads the news headlines, a dangerous war in the Middle East or floods in some part of the world that is still 'home' to a large part of the school's population.

How can schools acknowledge the emotional significance of these events without becoming overwhelmed by them? How can they help staff and young people experience the sort of calm states that enable them to maintain the bridge between their thinking and feeling? And how can they do so in a way that encourages a focus on learning?

Case studies 4 and 5 describe how teachers in respectively a primary and secondary school discovered that spending a few minutes, at the beginning of the school day or after a break, for their students to acknowledge their feelings and deal with what was happening for them enabled them to shift into emotional states more conducive to learning.

The lessons of reflection

These teachers were giving their students the opportunity to let go of their tensions and move out of emotional states that were not conducive to their learning. They did so not by telling them to be quiet – which might have provoked defiance – but by creating the sort of calm atmosphere that would make it possible for their moods to shift.

In doing this, they showed young people how they could develop their own capacity for managing emotional states. While we cannot consciously control our emotions, we can do things with our bodies (like breathing in a particular way or sitting in a different position) and to the environments in which we place ourselves (like sitting in a different position, looking at something colourful or putting on some music) that will modulate the way we are feeling.

p.25

This capacity to transform feelings is enormously useful in fostering **learning power**. By becoming more emotionally fluent, students can find ways of putting themselves into the sort of states that are most appropriate for whatever task they are engaged in – whether it is trying to analyse a problem, absorb masses of information, write an essay, prepare for an exam or come up with a creative idea.

Also, by creating opportunities for young people to go inside their own experience, to think about it, to value it and then to transform it, these teachers were helping them to see how they could come to know their emotions and formulate a language with which to build their learning relationships.

Some schools have found that it is useful to set up special rooms – Quiet Rooms – where young people, particularly those who are distressed or hyped up, can go to experience different emotional states. The room is equipped and decorated in a way that offers students who are finding it hard to cope with the ordinary pressures of school life the possibility of experiencing peace and tranquillity.

Case study 4

Giving a primary class time to focus

Sam and Eric have just had a go at each other in the playground. They are being escorted into class by the senior lunch supervisor. Another child, Suzy, is standing next to me and sobbing. Everyone, she tells me, hates her. The afternoon does not look promising. Emotions are spiralling out of control. I need to restore calm and a sense of purpose.

I ask the pupils to sit down. 'Either close your eyes or focus on a spot on the floor and be very still.' I quietly explain that I want to give everyone the opportunity to calm down and to make the right choices. Some children, I suggest, are about to make choices that will make them feel miserable. Within minutes, the atmosphere of the class has changed. The tension has gone. People are calm.

I pose some questions to the children. 'Think of a pleasant moment at playtime. Why did it feel good? What did you do to make it enjoyable? Was today's play as good? Why? If not, how could you have acted differently?'

I finish the reflection on a positive note by asking the pupils to feel the joy of love and friendship, whether from another child, parent or adult. After a concluding moment of stillness, the children open their eyes. They are now more relaxed, focused and in control of their emotions, ready to concentrate on their afternoon lessons.

This process takes about two to three minutes and has a dramatic impact upon the class. It gives the children a chance to enter their inner worlds and to explore their actions and feelings. Without others judging them, they are more likely to be honest with themselves, to learn about themselves, to gain control over their emotions and to refocus their thoughts in a positive way.

Karen Errington (Windmill First School, Oxfordshire)

Case study 5

Fostering calm before taking the register in a secondary classroom

The students are coming up the stairs to my room. It is a Year 11 class. I have taught Years 7 and 9 already today. Over lunch it will be homework, detentions and, after that, Year 11 again. I hear murmurs of 'Hello, miss' and a few eyes meet mine at the door.

I am tired and feel in need of strength to face this bubbling and energetic group. I may have to be very firm, and I know I cannot win them all, but I want to get the best out of them and for them to get the best out of me.

Inside the room, I am faced with a choice. Before we start, do I fulfil the school uniform policy and nag them about shirts, ties and baseball caps? Do I give out books and see the eyes hunt for the grade – ignoring the helpful comment I wrote? Will I get into the wearisome round of 'Everyone stop talking' and have to work very hard to draw them into the world of thought, without getting irritated and frustrated myself?

Instead, I try this start to my lesson.

Before bringing the students into the room, I put on music. The tables are empty. They will find no distraction when they come in. On the board I may have written a values word such as 'respect' or 'tolerance'. Maybe I have put up a statement: 'It is human to ask questions.'

I take a deep breath and open the door. As they enter, I try to meet everyone's eyes, mentioning many by name, and using words like 'Welcome, come in and get comfortable.' As the pupils sit down, I move around the room and talk quietly to each, over their chatter, asking them again to make themselves comfortable and to settle down. The chatter turns to 'What's that noise? We thought you had a choir in the room, miss!'

I will not tackle uniform and hats yet. I will not give them the books yet. Gradually, the chatter stops and the music quietly dominates. I return to the front and sit down.

As I gaze around the students, my first words are 'It's good to see you all.' I ask the class to try to get as comfortable in the chairs as they can and to listen to the music. I ask a pupil to put a focus time label on the door. This asks visitors to wait for two or three minutes before coming in. I talk so that they can hear me. If necessary, the music is turned down a little. I tell them I want them to feel relaxed – despite the rushed and busy day they have had. I tell them that our lesson is a time to share ideas, to reflect and to think about life. I may, at this point, refer briefly to the topic we are going to cover.

I then encourage them to relax their breathing by asking them (without noise) to breathe in for a count of four and out for four, and we all listen to the music for 30 seconds or so.

The room becomes very calm. I begin talking quietly, over the music, reminding them of the good things we have done in previous lessons. I point out their skills and their strengths; for example, the way they feel happy to speak and share, the way they will try to find different points of view. I encourage them to think of their contribution as positive – even behaviour like calling out in discussions is positive because it reflects their energy and interest.

Then I talk in more detail about the lesson and the skills they are going to use. I encourage them to think about how they are going to change each other's lives by the ideas they will talk about and the way they will be thinking. This time of reflection is creating a positive feeling and cohesive mood.

I invite them to use the remaining minute to relax and listen to the music, before we energise into the lesson.

At this point, I either let them sit and listen to the music, or I start quietly to give out books and lesson equipment. The murmur of chat begins to grow but I do not have to force my presence on it. I am in charge. Where possible, I do not argue and do not let my voice say things in a negative way.

Now I can begin the routine of register and uniform. The focus time label is removed. The mood has altered subtly. They are tuned in, I am relaxed and, whatever else may happen, we have had a positive start to the lesson. The value of the individual and the strengths of the group have been the focus of the first five minutes.

Alison Williams (Bartholomew Secondary School, Eynsham)

I just want to ask ...

Do you not realise that I would make myself the laughing stock of the school if I were to start asking my students to sit down quietly and listen to New Age music?

Sometimes you really do have to try something to see the way it works. We are so concerned to ensure that every minute of every day is used to accomplish specific tasks that we can overlook the need to make sure that those minutes are used to maximum effect. Stilling exercises like those described above help every member of the class get into the sort of emotional state that helps them to learn – to absorb information, generate ideas and collaborate with others. If it works, what does it matter how it looks or how other people judge it?

Useful reading

Farrer, F. (2000) *A Quiet Revolution: Encouraging Positive Values in Our Children.* London: Rider.

The story of the development of values education at West Kidlington Primary School shows how the reflective exploration of concepts such as honesty, truthfulness, respect, happiness, peace, responsibility and love helped children develop the inner confidence to deal with complex situations from a position of strength.

Hawkes, N. (2003) *How to Inspire and Develop Positive Values in Your Classroom.* Cambridge: LDA.

Written by a senior adviser in Oxfordshire who was formerly head at West Kidlington Primary and Nursery School, this book provides practical strategies for enabling teachers to promote positive values in their school by modelling a reflective attitude.

Taking an interest in what people are feeling

Emotional literacy requires us to take an interest in what happens between ourselves and others. What is this feeling that makes me uncomfortable? In what way is it a response to how the person over there is looking at me? What does he or she mean to communicate and what would be an appropriate way to react?

We all start out in life intensely curious about people and things, but gradually lose much of our wholehearted eagerness to explore. We learn to feel ashamed of the things we do not know, that we have to prove we are as good as our colleagues even though we fear that we are not. We find ourselves caught up in anxiety that we will never achieve the sense of mastery we long for. Finding it difficult to accept our ignorance and incompetence, we easily convince ourselves that we are not interested in knowing more.

But behind our apparent disinterest there is usually an intense curiosity waiting to be re-ignited, particularly about other people. Young people sit in their classrooms wondering why their peers respond to them as they do, what drives the ways in which their teachers behave, why the systems that govern their lives have been set up as they are. Case study 1 about a Year 9 class unable to listen to their teachers or to each other showed the enormous value of creating a context in which these questions could be opened up.

The blocking of this curiosity undermines the quality of learning in several different ways. It leaves people stuck in troubled emotional states where they cannot concentrate, take in information or focus on tasks. It does not address the need for young people to find ways of knowing more about each other if they are to work collaboratively together. It closes off the possibility of this emotional knowledge being applied in their learning, and it prevents them exploring topics in a way that might provoke difficult emotional states they have no way of handling.

As described more fully in a later section on the **curriculum**, this capacity to ask p.69 ▷ questions about what is happening emotionally within the learning group has enormous potential for enriching the study of academic subjects. Whether what is being explored is a literary narrative, a historical event or a scientific discovery, deploying the emotional understanding contained within the group equips students to think much more richly about the interplay of characters and contexts involved in whatever they are studying.

By re-engaging their curiosity, by declaring that it is okay to ask whatever questions call for attention, to seek for reasons that will explain the way things are, to share with each other what they perceive, to hunt out information that will supplement what they already know, teachers and other staff enable students to transform themselves from recipients of knowledge into active agents in its discovery and creation.

Challenging assumptions

This perspective does not fit with the idea that people need to be driven to learn, and that knowledge should be 'transmitted'. Case study 6 describes Carrie Winstanley's experience as she introduced a group of student teachers to **Philosophy for Children (P4C)**. She encountered a lot of scepticism about whether p.65 ▷ children who were usually incapable of working together could join in framing and exploring questions. In each case, they were surprised at how far the nature of the task stimulated young people's engagement.

The reason young people respond so well to opportunities for engaging collaboratively in thinking about questions and then following where they lead is because they *want* to find answers. Their questions emerge out of experience and, in their minds, there is no firm dividing line between those questions that are about self and relationships, and those that are about the wider world. In allowing them to pursue these questions, teachers show respect for their students and a belief in their capacity to find answers. Such attitudes energise the desire to learn.

What those who dismiss this sort of approach usually miss is the collaborative learning energy that is generated when a group of young people start to act together upon their desire to know and understand. As they exchange ideas and discover more about each other, they stimulate their capacity to think, reflect and investigate. Curiosity is the engine of learning. By resisting the understandable impulse to provide answers and to tell young people what they need to know, we allow them to make fresh discoveries and to open up original channels of enquiry.

Case study 6

Helping student teachers let young people set the agenda

Carrie Winstanley, a lecturer at the University of Surrey, Roehampton, asked a group of her students to run a session, or series of sessions, creating their own materials for using P4C. Students' reflections proved most interesting as many moved from a sceptical view to a position of strong support for the use of the approach. This is how she reported on the experience of five of those students.

Pippa

As a teacher of nursery children, Pippa was in control of the format, structure and length of the sessions and had a good knowledge of the pupils. She felt that children would not really be interested in issues outside of the storybook she chose for her session.

> This was the first time I let the children set the agenda and I found it really difficult to let go of my usual amount of control. Once I managed to loosen up, the children really got into the swing of things. Their discussion was more wide-ranging than I could have imagined.

Debbie

Debbie was surprised by the enthusiasm with which normally reticent children approached the task and were willing to open up.

> I was amazed at a couple of girls who had not made a peep all term. They seemed to blossom when they were allowed to decide what they wanted to talk about.

Debbie has been appointed as a full-time classroom assistant in the school where she undertook her study and is planning to make the sessions an important part of her work.

Nick

Nick was nervous about approaching this work with children:

> My lot are used to me doing football training and mucking about. I'm not sure if they'll go for picture books.

A lively group of nine-year-old boys surprised Nick by choosing to focus on some profound themes.

> Once we had got some silliness out of the way, they really wanted to talk about what friendship really means. How does an argument affect the way you feel about your friends? How can you tell someone what you feel without hurting them? Issues like that.

Karen

As a mature student already working in a school, Karen planned something far more elaborate. Already convinced of the benefits of P4C for younger children, she decided to create some materials for secondary school pupils in a local school where a friend was struggling with children exhibiting challenging behaviour. She planned materials for teachers and children and thoughtfully produced them as audio cassettes to allow teachers to receive training while on the move, and to allow for minimal preparation time when teachers merely needed to find the right spot on a cassette and press 'play'.

> It took a lot of convincing but teachers were gushing in their praise of the effects of the sessions. They have asked for me to come back and help them out some more, which is great considering it implies extra work for them and they are no different from other exhausted teachers.

Kelly

Kelly was very sceptical about the whole process. Once persuaded that her picture book ideas were appropriate, she reluctantly ran the first session in the classroom. It was reasonable but she was still rather demotivated and I had to try hard to convince her to go through with the second session. Seeing as half the work had been done, she agreed it was worth a go but managed to arrange the session to run at a time that meant she missed a college lecture. This was a deliberate ploy to test how much I wanted her to go into school, but I was pleased to let her skip the lecture and was more than delighted with the eventual results. The session was a great success and despite herself Kelly came back to class brimming with enthusiasm.

> My class teacher said she was impressed with the way the children were buzzing with ideas and really engaged with the picture book. Children who had refused to sit next to each other and work in cooperative groups were engaged in animated discussion and were managing to express their disagreement with one another without becoming aggressive or taking criticism personally.

I just want to ask …

Don't children need to acquire a significant body of knowledge before they start exploring their feelings about a topic?

Of course young people need knowledge; in fact they are often hungrier for it than we quite recognise. There really is no controversy here and yet it is an argument that gets put quite a lot. How, people say, can you discuss the French revolution or Newton's second law of motion unless you have a full grasp of what you are talking about? The issue is whether we are willing to tolerate the fact that young people may find themselves sharing lots of half-understood and partly digested pieces of information. This leads some people to the conclusion that we need to cram their heads full of the correct data before allowing them to reflect together. We at Antidote, by contrast, think that allowing people to share their unreliable knowledge builds their capacity to think rigorously and creatively. In the process, they will learn about how different people see the world and develop ways of establishing how to assess the reliability of what they pick up.

But the curriculum isn't going to go away. How can we allow children's minds to wander in whatever direction takes their fancy?

We are not denying the value of having a curriculum, but saying that it is important to give time for exploration and enquiry alongside more traditional modes of teaching. Young people do not necessarily need to be told what they need to learn in order to learn it. The advantages of giving them the opportunity to find their own way to the material enormously outweigh the risks involved in not prescribing the path they have to go down to get there.

Engaging in dialogue

As people learn to put their feelings into words, to experience more fully what they are feeling and to talk with each other about what is going on between them, they become ready to engage in dialogue, a conversation animated by participants' commitment to appreciating the thoughts and feelings of each other. It is through dialogue that emotional literacy develops and makes its contribution to learning.

Dialogue involves teachers and students speaking together about what it is that they are thinking and feeling. They could be talking about a new topic in science, a book they have read, an incident in the playground, the reason why they are feeling nervous about an upcoming exam or whatever else. Dialogue does not involve particular skills or techniques, just a genuine interest in one's fellow participants.

Making dialogue possible

Dialogue gives its participants an opportunity to understand their own experience by reflecting on it in the company of others. It becomes possible when those who take part feel able to talk together as if they were equals, when they know they are not going to be judged or directed towards a defined goal.

Dialogue frees people from their concern about how others will see them. Assured that what they say will be valued and appreciated, they sense that their opinions can be heard and that it will be possible to explore collectively what is going on between them.

The responsibility for whoever facilitates the process is to ensure that people experience the group as a place of safety, so that they have the confidence to speak freely, to hear what others are saying and to engage in a process of learning through the sharing of feelings and thoughts.

This involves establishing agreement on the basic principles that will govern the way people communicate with each other – such as not judging other people's comments, asking questions about the assumption underlying what has been said and listening very carefully – then ensuring that these principles are applied.

Also important is the need to keep on renegotiating these principles so as to ensure that people feel that the process continues to engage them, and responds to what is happening emotionally.

When dialogue works, its participants experience a growing freedom to say what it is that intrigues, perplexes or worries them; to use their own insights and imagination in the development of shared understanding. As they exchange their thoughts and feelings, they start to broaden the range of what they can say, and to understand more about themselves as well as others. This broader understanding of others' experience helps them to tolerate the emotions they once found difficult to endure and to think across a broader canvas.

What happens in dialogue

Dialogue enables young people and their teachers to test out their ideas to see how they resonate with, and differ from, those of others. Participants open themselves to the inner experience of others – how they respond to situations, how they see themselves, how they view the world around them.

It is the openness of the interchange that gives dialogue its potential to engage, excite and stimulate, deepening insight as well as depth and complexity in thinking. It also creates the possibility that something can happen in the interchange to shift the views people hold, the way they live their lives, their working models of relationships or whatever else.

Julia Ipgrave is a teacher and researcher who uses dialogue in her religious education classes to provide children with a forum in which they can develop the skills needed to face difference and adapt to continuing change. She is based in Leicester, a city where ethnic minorities make up 50 per cent of children in primary schools.

One of the most exciting discoveries of her research into children's religious understanding has been the extent to which dialogue is already taking place. The coexistence of different religions and views of the world has caused children to ask each other questions about the various ways in which God is understood and worshipped. This interest waits to be channelled towards understanding.

Her work also shows how cognitive and emotional questions become interwoven in children's conversations. This was very clear in a discussion that Ipgrave ran with three Year 6 children on how the world began. They had been sharing their understanding of what happened when Adam and Eve disobeyed God's instruction not to eat the apple from the tree of knowledge when a Rastafarian boy known as a troublemaker in the school asked a question about what would happen to the world when God stopped making people. A Hindu girl sitting with him picked up on the idea that God might be getting bored.

At this point JH said something enormously powerful that emerged from the inner dialogue that had been going on in his head: 'I wish I was a little baby again – start all over again – start my life again. Start to behave myself because it's too late now.'

'I don't think it's too late when you're 11 years old,' his teacher responded.

'I'm going to secondary school,' JH carried on, 'I know I'm going to do that, but I want to start over again at infant school and behave myself all the way through.'

Dialogue had created the conditions that allowed JH both to have this feeling/thought and to share it with his peers. What he said made links to a number of different ideas that were being discussed. Talk about the beginning of the world linked into his awareness that he had lived the beginning phase of his life. Reflecting on what was forbidden by God made him think about his own (mis)behaviour. Where Adam and Eve had been expelled from Eden, he was threatened with exclusion from school. And he was now about to make a transition to secondary school, as they had made the transition into the human world.

It is because dialogue allows these sorts of links to be made, savoured and explored as part of the learning task that it fosters the capacity to find links and forge meaning. It is a process that brings to the discussion the content from several layers of the mind, and allows people to work collaboratively on pulling them together and making something out of them.

As Zoe Donoahue says in case study 7 about her experience of getting primary students to engage in dialogue on their reading, most classroom conversation is not dialogue (and the same is true of conversations in the wider world). People have prepared positions to put across and all too rarely respond in what they say to what has just been said. By removing themselves from an interactive process, they limit the possibilities of what can happen between them.

Donoahue's response was to tell her students that they could only speak if their comments built directly on the latest statement. They quickly picked up the idea that they needed to listen more attentively to each other and to refer back what they were saying to the previous speaker's comments. In the process, they started to learn as much from each other as they did from their teachers.

Teachers encourage dialogue by:

- being attentive to what is happening between young people as they engage in dialogue – where their thinking is coming from, how they are relating to each other and what ideas are emerging;
- encouraging young people to given reasons for what they say and to ask questions when they do not understand or want to know more;
- relaxing their control of the content of the discussions and being ready to be taken in surprising new directions by the children's contributions;
- adopting a facilitative role that involves helping the dialogue along without taking over, ensuring that individuals do not dominate the process, nor are they sidelined;
- being ready to handle controversial, damaging and sensitive statements.

Thanks to Julia Ipgrave for contributing these points

Case study 7

How young people can develop their own rules to govern the dialogue between them

I have always allowed ample time for discussion after reading to the class. I believe that it helps children to better understand the text on a basic level, as well as encouraging them to examine characters and their motivations, make predictions, discuss the author's style and choices, and explore the characteristics of various genres of writing.

Our discussions were lively, but something was lacking. I was bothered by the disjointed quality of our talk. One child would make a comment, and the next child's comment would bear no relationship to what the first had said. Sometimes we would come back to the same topic, or thread, some minutes later, but there would be no development of ideas; the discussions consisted of isolated comments. As well, I felt I needed to validate each child's comment by saying something afterwards. The effect of these practices was to leave me in control of the discussion.

Early in the school year, I talked to the children about my concerns. A new format was proposed. To begin, I would choose one child who had his or her hand raised. If someone had something to say that related to or built upon that comment, he or she could speak next without raising his or her hand. Similarly, if the next person's comment was related, they too could speak without being chosen by me. We would continue in this way until that particular idea, or thread, had been exhausted. I would then choose another child from those who had their hands raised, and a new thread would begin.

After years of needing permission to talk in a discussion, some children were hesitant to speak out without being chosen or hearing what I thought of the previous comment. Soon, though, most were jumping in themselves. Quite spontaneously they started to preface their ideas with expressions such as, 'This goes with Chris's comment', 'I agree with Lauren', 'I sort of agree with Petra, but I sort of don't.' These comments demonstrated that they were listening well and making a conscious link between their thoughts and the ideas of their peers.

Despite the success of our new format, I still found that children looked to me for my reaction after each comment, rather than focusing on the person who was talking. As a result, I told them that I would look down when children talked. This seemed to help.

A further step would be to remove myself completely from the circle, giving total control of the discussion to the children. However, this would remove the opportunity to model appropriate comments and behaviour. It is a step I would not undertake until the children's discussion skills were at quite a high level.

My goal is to talk as little as possible, and to wait until well into the discussion before making comments. A great deal of teaching can occur through the teacher's judicious participation. Before I speak, I try to have in mind not only what I will say, but why I am saying it. Not only do I try to expand the children's repertoire of comments, but I consciously echo the types of comments they are making in order to reinforce what they are doing well.

Clearly, the relationship between teachers and learners is not a dialogue between equals, as the teacher needs to take on the role of leader and guide to ensure that the students engage with the mandated curriculum, and that they are assisted to appropriate it as effectively as possible. To this end, I cannot remain silent, but must make comments and ask questions that provide scaffolding as the younger, less experienced members of the community learn to take part in discussions.

After the discussion is over, I am more direct in my teaching, commenting briefly on how the discussion went that day, what was successful and what I would like them to think about for next time. As well, I might explain the motivation behind something that I did or said during the discussion.

Zoe Donoahue (1998)

I just want to ask ...

Doesn't this approach undervalue what teachers know and have to contribute?

We would say that it suggests different ways in which teachers' knowledge and experience can be employed. Clearly, it is enormously important that teachers show young people that it is possible to know, that they share with them the pleasure they take in learning and that they make themselves available to help students understand things they cannot grasp on their own. Dialogue-based approaches are ways of using individual knowledge and authority to stimulate young people's energy for learning without the risk of dampening down their curiosity.

Evidence for the value of dialogue

Through researcher observation over eight weeks, it was shown that recall of the content of units about ancient Egyptian society by Grade 8 students was greater when 'dialogic instruction' was inherent in the lessons. The researchers meant by this substantive conversation which was more coherent, sustained, thematic and in-depth than 'traditional' teaching.

In dialogic classrooms, students were engaged in classroom discourse about important academic topics in the texts they were reading. More time was allocated to collaboration rather than routine teaching. And the teacher regularly focused on how to learn as well as on the content of the lessons.

As the weeks went on, collaborative discourse allowed students to initiate major topics and questions; a larger variety of forms of discourse were co-constructed with the students; content learning was built into learning about learning.

Aulls (1998)

Evolving personal narratives

Dialogue puts us in touch with the ways in which people affect each other. This information becomes built into the stories that we tell ourselves to explain the patterns of our own lives: why particular actions have consequences and what the answers are to such basic questions as: What am I doing here? How do I fit in here? Where do I want to go from here? Do I want to learn these things?

We described earlier how we build around the experiences we have of others the 'working models' that shape the way we behave in particular situations. These models are narratives we use to tell ourselves who we are and how others view us. All emotional experience has a history. Whether we are shocked, enchanted or terrified by a particular event will reflect how previous related experiences have affected us.

It is clearly very important what stories are triggered in the classroom and the school. How we relate to teachers and whether we are able to learn anything might depend on whether we use a story about how the person who tells me my work is not as good as it might be thinks I am stupid and wants me to fail, or a story about how the person speaking to me in this way thinks I could do better and is willing to help me succeed.

Even if particular patterns become more firmly established than others, everyone develops a range of such working models. If they are to learn better or behave differently, they need to find models that help them navigate the situation in which they find themselves. What helps them to achieve this task?

How stories change us

If we are to understand what we are feeling, we need to grasp the narrative history that lies behind our emotional state. In recognising the different interpretations we can put upon that history, we start to see how we can reshape the way we handle our emotions and our responses to others. We start to see our own role in events in relation to other people's, begin to understand the complexity of our own experience and to appreciate the way other people conduct themselves.

This perspective on the importance of narrative is supported by research into the transmission of parenting patterns across generations. What enables people to break out of dysfunctional ways of relating to others they have learned early on is an ability to build a coherent narrative of their experience. The process of doing this involves them in rebuilding the **bridge between thinking and feeling**. It is when the facts about what has happened get packaged up with the feelings that people can start to tell clear and consistent stories about who they are and where they come from. This opens up the possibility of being able to make real choices about how to deal with particular situations.

The four processes we have described in this section so far – developing a language for feelings, reflecting on feelings, taking an interest in feelings, engaging in dialogue – support people in processing emotional experience so that their feelings can be thought about and their thinking can be enriched by feeling. The next step is to foster people's capacity to shape and develop the stories they tell about themselves.

There are many stories told in our schools. Literary narratives are explored alongside stories about the workings of power in history and of exploration in science. Key events from last night's soaps are exchanged for gossip about teachers or fellow students. Practising emotional literacy involves finding ways to enrich the understanding of these narratives about the world outside by setting them in relationship to the narratives of individual learners' lives: in this way allowing the stories we tell about the world to enrich our understanding of ourselves, and the stories we tell about ourselves to infuse academic study.

Linda Bausch (2001) is a literacy specialist at Long Island University in New York. Her main field of interest lies in 'the depth of understanding and connection a reader can create when encouraged to develop a personal relationship with the text'.

One day she was working with a nine-year-old student called Terry whose grades marked her down as a struggling reader and writer. The book they were reading was called *Night of the Twisters* and they had come to a section of the story where the main character's father had picked up his son by the arm and dropped him in anger over a bicycle which he had left outside. Linda and Terry paused for a moment to discuss what had just occurred in the story. When asked what she was thinking, Terry replied that she did not feel comfortable with the father being angry in the story. It reminded her of her grandfather, how he had slapped her in the face because he thought she was allowing her nose to run on purpose.

p.14

As they spoke, Linda discovered the deep and complex meaning that Terry had discovered in the story. She had connected the narrative to her own life, linking the violence of the character in the story to her personal experience with violence. In the process, Linda had discovered both a way to engage Terry more actively in the practice of reading, and the depth of her capacity to think about the meaning of a particular literary narrative. There was, in short, a degree of learning power available, that could be released by allowing Terry to more fully engage her emotional experience in the process of reading.

The more students can be encouraged to bring their emotional understanding to their reading and writing, the more engaged they will be by the process and the richer will be the work they produce. Matt Chappel, the deputy head of Star Primary in Canning Town, seeks to develop a workshop atmosphere in his classrooms where students can reflect on their feelings and use those reflections in their fiction. He takes young people through visualising and brainstorming exercises to think about the settings of their stories; role-play to explore emotional responses to different personalities; and mood-mapping to track the way emotions shift in narrative. By focusing on the experience, rather than words, sentences and paragraphs, he enables them to write much more interesting narratives.

Being the author of your own life

People naturally become more involved in stories that they can relate to their own lives. They recognise situations that they have been in, feelings that they have experienced and the many different ways in which these can affect us. But it is also true that when people explore the stories they read with others whom they know and care about, they find different ways to perceive these narratives, different ways of become engaged in the dilemmas and questions they throw up. They steadily enlarge their sympathetic imagination, the range of what they can understand and take an interest in.

The importance of sharing personal narratives so that people can build a stronger sense of themselves inspired a project that Anne Murray and Jane Law ran at Central Foundation Girls' School in London. They were working with girls from Years 8 to 10 who were seen as lacking self-belief, motivation or the capacity to learn independently.

The project was called 'Being the author of your own life' and drew on the work of two Australian social workers, Michael White and David Epsom, whose approach was based on the belief that, for people to develop resilience, it was important for them to:

- know that they had a story that was theirs to tell;
- know that being aware of how your story is developing is how you develop your identity;

- believe that their story was as important as anyone else's;
- believe that they needed to keep track of that story;
- recognise that their identity could be accessed far more easily through their story than through conscious thoughts, or through what other people might try to tell them about themselves.

Over successive sessions, the girls worked with the stories of various fictional characters, reflected privately on their own stories, shared the thoughts that came out of these reflections with colleagues and then worked up what emerged from these discussions through dialogue, drama exercises and imaginative games. There then followed a series of workshops looking at issues such as conflict, emotional awareness and empathy.

We wanted the students to come out at the end of this experience with a belief that their stories were completely valid and important. A belief in one's capacity to 'author' one's story is a way into developing emotional and moral and spiritual resilience.

Stories help us to:

- reflect on our own emotions
- understand the consequences of our actions
- know ourselves
- reflect on the emotions of others
- develop empathy for others
- acknowledge difference

I just want to ask ...

Aren't you likely to confuse people by inviting them to make links between their own lives and the lives of the people they are studying?

This is not something you have to invite people to do. It is something that goes on in the back of people's heads much of the time. We have an enormous capacity to relate our own experience to that of peoples in other cultures, social groups and historical periods. By making this explicit, you both enrich the discussions that go on and clarify any confusions between personal experience and whatever is being studied.

3

Contexts

Talking together

If young people are to develop the elements of emotional literacy described in the previous chapter, it helps if they can practise dialogue within every school activity.

Circle time, peer support and therapeutic group work are processes currently practised in our schools which have clear value as opportunities for young people to process difficult feelings, explore emotional experience and evolve more effective ways of relating to each other.

They do not represent the totality of ways in which young people can be encouraged to talk about aspects of their relationships to each other, nor do they in themselves necessarily promote emotional literacy. That depends on factors such as the quality of their facilitation and the atmosphere of the school.

Dialogue can enrich learning in a physics or maths lesson. The more, indeed, it can permeate every element of the curriculum, the more it enables students to engage their emotional understanding in thinking and learning.

If schools are to take student participation seriously, they need to encourage young people to reflect on the feelings that emerge as they share views on how discipline is delivered, how the lunch queue is managed, who delivers the curriculum and everything else. By doing so, they will become better able to understand why different people say different things, to reconcile differences, to negotiate conflicts and to create the conditions for the emergence of a healthy learning community in their schools.

For teachers and other school staff promoting dialogue in all these areas, handing over to young people responsibility for developing their agenda, involves helping them find ways to share with each other the different things they know, feel or think, seeking for information that will answer the questions which come up, exploring freely the ideas that come up and, through this process, generating new understanding.

This involves developing a form of authority that is based in their capacity to demonstrate they have already engaged with these questions, thought about them, developed ways of managing them, that they have, moreover, the generosity to help learners without imposing upon them, to willingly provide support when it is asked for, to guarantee that things will not get out of hand or decline into apathy.

Practising emotional literacy creates an environment in the classroom and in the rest of the school that enables young people to become active agents in the acquisition, development and management of knowledge about all sorts of things. It encourages them to engage in dialogue by shaping questions around what interests them, and exploring these collaboratively with their peers.

Circle time

Circle time is based on a long tradition of people sitting down in a circle to think about the life of their community. It provides opportunities to address shared issues and to experience what it means to be part of a group. In a circle, children and young people can experience themselves as holding the authority and insight to manage their own relationships.

Circle time approaches generally contain some combination of:

- processes for establishing ground rules, such as taking turns, listening attentively, being polite;
- sanctions to be applied when people ignore these basic principles;
- games designed to energise young people, get them feeling comfortable and safe with each other and generally promote a positive atmosphere;
- opportunities to explore emotions and the actions that flow from them.

Circle time has the potential to create the conditions of safety that allow young people to express thoughts, feelings, hopes and fears; to face their differences and share common experiences. It can help to stimulate dialogue, to foster a sense of collective well-being and to shape common understandings that have the capacity to flow out of the circle into the whole of young people's lives, enabling them, through increased understanding, to take on more responsibility for themselves, their behaviour and their learning.

If it is to achieve this, the various elements of circle time need to be integrated in a way that stimulates participation and draws children into caring for and supporting each other.

In case study 8, Helen Moss and Valerie Wilson (1998) describe their experience of introducing circle time to a Year 6 class. They discovered that it allowed things to be said that would not have emerged in any other context. Keys to its

success were the opportunities for real participation and the way in which the teachers' perspective was present so as to allow it to be taken in and thought about. Moss and Wilson credit the process with reducing the number of disruptive playground incidents, increasing engagement in class discussions and broadening the range of pupils' friendship.

Circle time is more common in primary schools than in secondary, but this has more to do with the tightness of the timetable and the way teachers' relationships with students are constructed than with any inherent difficulties in applying the approach with secondary students. Case study 9 recounts how 13-year-old Dean benefited from the experience of being able to discuss in a circle why he was in trouble so much of the time.

Evidence for the value of circle time

An evaluation of a Quality Circle Time programme for Year 7 students at Headlands School in Wiltshire concluded that it was successful in enabling pupils to:

- reflect on their behaviour;
- set targets for improvements;
- regulate their personal behaviour;
- acquire skills and attitudes relevant to positive peer relationships;
- become more sensitive to, and tolerant of, others;
- develop skills in attending, observing, thinking, speaking and listening.

The researchers also reported a development in perceived self-efficacy. Those who took part in the programme were pleased to report that they had overcome some of their reluctance to express opinions and tell others about themselves. The spirit of cooperation was said to have generalised to behaviour in classrooms and schools more generally.

Robinson and Tayler (1999)

Case study 8

Two teachers describe how they set about investigating whether circle time could improve the atmosphere in their Year 6 class

We carried out a small-scale project over a period of ten weeks to investigate whether relationships between pupils in a Year 6 class could be improved through a tailor-made programme of PSE activities drawing on circle time. We were particularly interested in whether the programme made a difference to the classroom 'climate'.

As experienced Year 6 teachers with 17 years of teaching experience between us, we were surprised and disappointed by the relationships in our class. The issue that first brought the problem to our attention was lunch-time incidents between the pupils. It was a regular occurrence at the beginning of afternoon school for the lunch-time supervisor responsible for Year 6 to report on an argument or fight that had taken place between members of the class. The individuals involved were often very upset and many pupils in the class could be vociferous on the matter. The atmosphere at the beginning of afternoon school was not, therefore, conducive to a calm and friendly learning environment.

We found ourselves spending time before starting afternoon lessons in talking to the pupils involved and calming the class in general. We decided that something more structured and proactive on our part was required. We decided to run circle time sessions. These took the form of weekly 45-minute sessions where the whole class sat in a circle to participate in games, discussion, structured activities and role-play.

There were three 'golden rules': pupils could only speak when they had the 'magic object' (a conch shell) in their hands. They could say 'pass' if they had nothing to say, and there should be no put-downs.

We evaluated the effectiveness of the programme in two ways involving, firstly, deliberate and planned discussions between us as the two teachers and, secondly, asking the children to tell us about their impressions and friendship preferences. The information was examined using both qualitative and quantitative methods.

In our view, the sessions were successful because they had made clear to the pupils the type of positive responses that we, as their teachers, were trying to encourage, and the type of negative responses we considered unacceptable. Circle time had achieved this in a way that was fun and involved a great deal of pupil participation. We felt it had succeeded, due to this 'game' element, where moral lectures or quiet chats to individuals had failed.

There were obvious indications of more positive relationships between pupils such as the reduction in the number of playground incidents. There were also indications of an atmosphere of increased tolerance and empathy in the classroom. Pupils who had not previously participated in class discussions were more willing to join in. There were fewer put-downs and pupils seemed to make less fuss about whom they were asked to work with.

We expected that children's friendships would have widened and their willingness to work with other members of the classroom would have increased. To test this we adopted a sociometric measure that revealed significant differences in pupil preferences in terms of the number of pupils they were willing to mix with at break-time or work with in the classroom.

Moss and Wilson (1998)

Case study 9

How Dean benefited from circle time at his secondary school

Dean never meant to be in trouble. He was one of those 13-year-old boys who just does not think before he acts. His body was growing faster than his brain seemed able to register and his arms and legs seemed to have a life of their own. He tended to knock things over, make precipitate entries to rooms, run, jump and shout in corridors and playgrounds and more worrying than all of these, to do and say inappropriate things in all the wrong places. Consequently, whatever his intentions, he was in trouble much of the time.

Dean's tutor was fed up with having to tackle the catalogue of complaints that colleagues waited at the staffroom door to tell him each morning and Dean himself had detentions in his diary for weeks to come. School life was not much fun. In fact, the relentless sense of helplessness borne out of remorseless predictability led Dean to devise his own simple cure. He avoided the problems by skipping lessons.

It was at this point that a glimmer of light appeared on Dean's horizon. He was invited to attend a group called the 'Positive Choice Group'. He did not really know what that meant, but it sounded better than history, science or maths. Anyway, the person who was coming to the school each Tuesday to run the group seemed OK. She interviewed him to see if he would agree to a contract for taking part in the group. It involved meeting with the lady for half an hour on his own and then taking part in a small group that sounded a bit like his primary school experience of circle time. He discovered that several other members of Year 8 were being asked if they wanted to go, so maybe it would be a bit of a laugh. He knew that this group was to help him do better at school, so he was not surprised to find out that several other people he knew from the detention rota were also offered places. The curious bit was when he was asked if he could think of someone in his tutor group who hardly ever got into trouble and whom he liked who could also come to the group. He chose Stephen and, when Steve was asked if he would be a kind of mentor to Dean, he agreed.

The Positive Choice Group was scheduled for six consecutive weeks and with apprehension Dean approached his first individual session with the lady. It was OK. They talked about all kinds of things to do with his home life including his hobbies, likes and dislikes. He began to relax a little.

The group session was run by the same lady and a member of staff from the school. There were ten students and two adults. They all sat in a circle. The best bits were playing games, having a laugh and being given a chance to talk. They were not very good at the start of the group. They messed about and would not listen to each other. Gradually, though, they became more interested in the activities. There was so much to think about. They played problem-solving games where they had to all work together. They drew and did card-sorting exercises. They used Post-it notes to capture their ideas and at the end of every session they looked for things that had gone well and things that had changed since the last time they met. Dean noticed with interest that the people who had been chosen as mentors had difficulties just like the rest of them and some of the ones who were always in trouble could do some things better than the so-called good ones. This circle felt like a more level playing field than other lessons.

The biggest change came for Dean in one of his individual sessions. He had been thinking about his dearest ambition with the lady who ran the circles. They looked on the internet to see what qualifications were needed to be a fighter pilot and suddenly an awful reality dawned. Dean put his head in his hands and said, 'It's no good, I've been too bad. I've lost too much ground and I can't make it now, can I?' 'Why not?' came the unexpected reply. 'Of course you can make up for lost time. Of course you can realise your dream.' Dean grasped the hope offered to him and began to look for ways forward. He started to think about the obstacles that he put in his own path and those that he allowed other people to throw his way. Bit by bit, he thought of strategies to improve his behaviour and his achievement. He asked his parents for a maths tutor outside school and began to sit next to other people in class. He asked his mentor to sit next to him and to help him to stay out of trouble. Slowly things began to improve.

The Positive Choice Group only lasted six weeks, but it had a lasting impact for Dean. The next time it ran he mentored someone else in his class and helped them to get more out of school. It was not a miracle cure. Dean still found himself in plenty of scrapes including a short fixed-term exclusion for setting a gas tap alight in the science lab. He had many more strategies for dealing with the set-back, however, including a sense that he could make choices. His future seemed to have moved into his own hands and he no longer felt a victim at the receiving end of perceived injustice on the part of teachers or of inexplicable circumstances in school. He had more confidence and a greater sense of purpose.

Marilyn Tew
marilyntew@btopenworld.com

Useful resources

Ballard, J. (1980) *Circlebook: a Leader Handbook for Conducting Circletime*. New York: Ardent Media Inc.

Ballard describes ten characteristics that define the ethos of circle time. He emphasises that circle time is not about solving problems but about building awareness. 'Circle time is an educational model,' he says, 'and belongs in a school curriculum along with other content areas. It requires no esoteric leader skills such as are required for counselling or doing therapy or treatment of any kind.'

Bliss, T., Robinson, G. and Maines, B. (1995) *Developing Circle Time*. Bristol: Lucky Duck Publishing.

Explores the impact that circle time can have on the development of social behaviours, ethics and morality and shows how issues starting outside the circle can be supported within the security of an already established circle group. Includes worksheets.

Mosley, J. (1993) *Turn Your School Around*. Cambridge: LDA.

Mosley describes a circle-time approach to the development of self-esteem and positive behaviour in the primary staffroom, classroom and playground. She provides materials relating to the development of a framework for a whole-school approach, sessions for head teachers, teachers and support staff, lunch-time policy, use in classroom and parental involvement.

Mosley, J. and Tew, M. (1999) *Quality Circle Time in Secondary Schools*. London: David Fulton.

This book makes a case for the rigour of quality circle time as an opportunity for students to talk openly on a range of issues within set rules. The authors show how circle time used consistently across a secondary school can enhance the ethos, leading to improved self-esteem and more self-led learning. There is a wide range of suggested activities and self-evaluation prompts.

See Appendix 2 for organisations promoting or offering training in circle time.

Peer support

Peer support involves young people being given structured opportunities to help each other deal with emotional and relationship issues. It covers a range of processes with different names – peer listening, peer befriending, peer mentoring, peer mediation, peer tutoring or peer advocacy. The aim in every case is to put young people in a position where they can take responsibility for the well-being of others like themselves, and in the process can create a more positive emotional climate in their schools.

Peer mediators, for example, invite students to bring their conflicts for resolution. They set up a safe environment for both parties and ask them to agree to a set of simple ground rules. After listening to each side of the story, they ask questions about the feelings and needs that are driving the situation, in an effort to work out a way to move things forward.

Peer support schemes use young people's interest in helping others and getting to know their peers as a way of enabling those who feel anxious, stressed and unhappy to find effective ways of transforming these feelings into more positive states. Although often seen as a strategy for tackling bullying, peer support can be an effective way of helping young people deal with a wide range of difficult emotional issues.

It is important that young people in a school experience any peer support scheme as genuinely addressing their own needs, rather than those defined for them by authority figures. This means that they need to have a role in shaping its management and also that the scheme must be understood and valued by the whole school community, as Netta Cartwright describes in case study 10.

Despite the name, peer support schemes usually involve older children seeking to buddy, mentor or mediate children in younger age groups. It offers those in the supportive role the opportunity to take responsibility for people who may look up to them, and to work out with them how to find a way through difficult situations.

Within peer support schemes, young people are empowered to use their own insights to come up with creative solutions to the problems that are brought to them, while working within a process that they have been trained to follow. The extent to which any peer support scheme can promote emotional literacy is largely dependent on whether or not it is embedded in a whole-school policy that encourages emotional openness.

Case study 10

Peer support at Walton High School in Staffordshire

Walton High School is a large comprehensive school with a mostly middle-class intake of about 1,200 students aged 11 to 18. It was one of the first schools in the UK to initiate a peer-support system.

In 1990, students from the school council agreed on the need to have a whole-school anti-bullying policy, a contract signed by all students, and a peer counselling service run by students. This policy was coordinated by an anti-bullying working party, which included students.

In 1995, the policy was formalised by the working party into a short written document to give the school's definition of bullying, to state current practice and to clarify future intentions. It is reproduced in the staff handbook and posted in classrooms and corridors along with procedures to be taken if people are bullied.

The peer-supporters, called 'buddies', have a total of seven days' re-evaluation counselling training on how to manage and release emotions, and provide a confidential listening and helping service. If students want help they can turn up at the weekly lunchtime 'drop-in' sessions and have a session in a private room. Buddies do not tell students what to do, but help them think of solutions and give support. They offer confidentiality unless they think a student's health, or somebody else's health, is in danger. They tell potential clients beforehand that a teacher would have to be told in that situation.

There are three ways in which students can get support from buddies:

- All year 7 tutor groups have two to four buddies who visit them once a week during a registration period. The buddies play self-esteem games with them and teach them some basic listening and co-counselling skills.
- Students from any year can ask a buddy directly for one-to-one counselling at the 'drop-in' or elsewhere. A poster of their names and photographs is placed inside the house office and in tutor rooms so that people can know who they all are and which tutor group they are in.
- If they prefer to keep their request for counselling secret, they can fill in a form beneath the problem box in the main entrance and post it in the box.

Students can arrange to have as many sessions as they like with their buddies. Outside of a session, the buddy will never mention the session. The buddies are closely supervised by the school counsellor and meet weekly for feedback and support.

Two surveys have shown that the peer support service has helped reduce bullying and improved the feeling of safety for students. Students interviewed used and appreciated the service and reported that the listening skills of the buddies helped them solve their problems. Students who had not used the service also appreciated it being there as it gave them a sense of security.

Netta Cartwright (2001, Peer Support Works)

Evidence for the value of peer support

Evaluations of peer support schemes repeatedly show:
- Increased confidence and self-esteem for both users and supporters
- Improved interpersonal and social skills for peer supporters
- Raised awareness of emotional health issues
- Better atmosphere in schools
- Better academic performance among teenage boys
- Greater pupil involvement in problem-solving

See Elizabeth Hartley-Brewer's book (below) for more information

Useful resources

Hartley-Brewer, H. (2003) *Stepping Forward: Working together through peer support*. National Children's Bureau.

This book clarifies the breadth and scope of peer support, and offers explanations of the different approaches. It provides a number of examples to demonstrate how peer support is being developed in different settings, and offers practical guidance for developing and implementing programmes.

McGowan, M. (2002) *Young People and Peer Support*. Brighton: Trust for the Study of Adolescence.

This provides supporting materials for setting up a peer support service with young people. It gives practical advice and guidance and includes: Setting up the infrastructure; Getting started; Recruitment; Training; Communication; Monitoring. It also considers common problems and provides a range of training materials.

Scherer-Thompson, J. (2002) *Peer Support Manual: A guide to setting up a peer listening project in education settings*. London: Mental Health Foundation.

This manual provides guidance for schools on setting up a peer listening service. Complete with case studies, handouts and training materials, it looks at the problems encountered in setting up a project, a training programme for peer listeners and support staff, issues of confidentiality and monitoring. Backed up by a video illustrating the work of four peer support schemes in secondary schools.

See Appendix 3 for organisations that promote or provide training in peer support.

Philosophy for children

P4C seeks to foster in children and young people the capacity to reason and think for themselves. Since it relies on young people using their own insights, and doing so in a collaborative way, the approach has the potential to foster emotional literacy. It enables students to find through their conversations different ways of knowing themselves and each other.

Teachers using P4C start by sharing a story or other stimulus (such as a poem, a painting or a piece of music) with a group of young people. They then ask them to come up with a series of questions about the material. These questions form the basis for one or more discussions in which the young people are encouraged to reflect more deeply and widely on both their thoughts and their feelings.

The spirit in a P4C session is one of open enquiry, where there are no right answers and every comment is looked at for its potential contribution to the discussion. Students are freed from the anxiety they might have about being judged so that they can pursue their intuitive hunches and creative imaginings in a playful spirit. This creates the possibility that the resulting exchanges will build emotional understanding.

p.4

The example of **Tuckswood First** showed the sort of learning energy that can be generated when young people are encouraged to draw on their own emotional knowledge for thinking, to drive the discussion and exchange ideas freely with each other. It also shows how questions about ideas or facts interweave with questions about people and their emotions.

In case study 11, James Nottingham describes the perceived benefits of a philosophy club at Tweedmouth First School. These included more positive interactions between students, a greater readiness to ask questions and an improved capacity to concentrate on lessons.

Case study 24 describes a project in Barrow set up to foster the social, emotional and cognitive development of young people. A subsequent development in this project has been the integration of philosophy for children as an approach that can contribute to helping staff and young people to reflect, collaborate, experience well-being and make wise choices.

Like circle time, P4C is more common in primary schools than secondary. But one High School in Cumbria uses enquiry as a major teaching and learning strategy through Key Stages 3, 4 and 5, and offers two lunch-time philosophy clubs. And at a High School in Northampton, thinking skills sessions are offered to all year groups in Key Stages 3 and 4, and there are experiments going on in the application of the approach to English, RE, art, geography, history and technology.

Case study 11
Philosophy for Children at Tweedmouth West First School

When Tweedmouth West carried out a self-esteem survey of children in Year 3, it found that of the 28 children in the class, seven boys had very negative attitudes towards school. They claimed, for example, not to like being asked to help the teacher – something that almost every other seven-year-old seems to like to do.

For two of the boys this was not unexpected. For the other five boys, the results came as a shock. Up until then, they had not displayed any behaviour to suggest they did not like school. They were not struggling academically, nor did they seem to have problems integrating; on the face of it they were happy.

The head teacher Brendan Malkin responded by asking staff to make a special point of praising these boys when they were achieving, and setting up an after-school Philosophy Club. The club was for any child in Year 3. The target group of boys were encouraged, but not required, to attend.

Of the seven boys identified by the survey, four attended the Philosophy Club on a regular basis, together with another seven classmates. The head teacher also ran P4C sessions during school time with the whole class. The failure of the other three boys to join the Philosophy Club was mainly explained by the unwillingness of their carers to pick them up later than 3.30pm.

Since the Philosophy Club began, the numbers attending regularly have risen to 25 children. All of the staff in the school have either done, or are about to do, an introductory P4C course. This means that all children in the school are now exposed to P4C sessions weekly (through class councils, which then feed into school councils every half-term, and Berwick town councils once a term).

The teachers at the school feel the philosophy lessons have had the following impacts:

- The children interact more positively with each other, are more willing to see other points of view, have a greater respect for each other, and are more supportive of other children.
- They are more ready to question each other, to question their teachers, and will ask more open and searching questions. When answering they will offer reasons without prompting.
- They can concentrate for longer, will stay on the thread of an argument/enquiry rather than going off at a tangent, and will home in on the key words/concepts without prompting.

James Nottingham (SAPERE)

Useful resources

Cam, P. (2002) *Thinking Together: Philosophical inquiry for the classroom*. Hale & Iremonger PTG Ltd (available from Bookstall Forum).

Shows how story-based material can be used to help children raise philosophical puzzles and problems that will set them thinking. It shows how to use questioning techniques, group discussion and other activities to develop thinking skills and concepts that can be applied across the curriculum particularly at Key Stages 2 and 3.

Splitter, L. J. and Sharp, A. M. (1995) *Teaching for Better Thinking: The classroom community of inquiry*. Australian Council for Education (available from Bookstall Forum).

Provides a detailed description of what philosophy offers to children and their teachers and what impact it is likely to have on the educational process and on personal, social and ethical development.

I just want to ask …

How do we persuade ourselves (and those to whom we answer) that time devoted to emotional literacy really is time well spent?

Time is clearly a real issue. Ultimately, we need to more fully recognise that the most valuable role for schools is to build young people's capacity to learn and enquire, and that teachers will be better able to play a full part in that if they are themselves doing the same at both an organisational and an academic level.

See Appendix 4 for organisations that provide training in Philosophy for Children.

Therapeutic group work

There are various reasons why some young people might feel unable to take an active part in the activities described in this section of the book. It may be that the experience of being respected, listened to and valued is too far from what they know in the rest of their lives for it to be comfortable in school. Or they may feel so exposed in the large group that their instinct is to flee or cause havoc.

p.34

Young people in this position need a safer environment in which to tackle these issues and to look for ways of making a connection to others. This is likely to involve them working in smaller groups, where there is more use of drama techniques such as those described in the section on developing **a language for feelings**, and more guidance from the teacher or facilitator about ways of dealing with difficult feelings.

In case study 12, Ye Min describes how he works, alongside another facilitator, with groups of eight children, offering them a range of opportunities to explore their feelings, their motivations for doing what they do and how they can start making their own choices about who they want to be.

Case study 12

Using therapeutic group work to help young people address the feelings that drive their actions

Observation 1

Seeing their real life stories enacted is a powerful tool for change. One Year 10 pupil told us a story in an early session, about how he smashed the windows of the school. He was able to 'direct' the action, see someone else portray his actions and observe what had happened, according to him. We were able to witness his anger and frustration at the school and the unsatisfactory way that the head teacher had dealt with the incident.

Observation 2

In another group, someone who had found it difficult to speak in the talking circle told us of various violent or intimidating experiences in which he had been involved, sometimes as the perpetrator. On previous occasions in the feedback diary that we use for further communication between facilitator and individual group members, he had only written one-word comments, such as 'OK' or 'Crap'. He was unhappy, obviously struggling in the group and I was concerned about him.

In week six, he mentioned a violent incident that had apparently begun when he started to verbally abuse somebody in a public place. This had resulted in him being hit by the person he had been verbally abusing. I started to direct the drama and had to ask a lot of questions to set the scene. This was not satisfactory, so he took over. He chose the people to be him, his opponent and the witnesses to the assault. The actors rehearsed the action and the dialogue. They began to adopt the correct roles for their characters. The rest of the group became engaged in the activity, which helped to ensure that the drama was enacted in a serious and meaningful way.

I was relieved that the incident did not glorify the verbal abuse or the violence. There was time for the group to reflect upon the reasons for the incident and why it had escalated. At the end of that session, the boy wrote, 'This has been a good session.' His quest in directing the drama allowed him to witness how the world saw him and his behaviours, and gave him an opportunity to reassess his actions.

Observation 3

Another group had been aware of a recent royal visit and, from the talking circle, we altered our usual warm-up games so that they were performed in the style of royalty (i.e. swap chairs like a king or queen, build a shed like a king or queen etc.).

The group then made drawings of their palaces and discussed what they would have in them. In subsequent weeks we created an imaginary island and placed the palaces on its landscape. A carriage was created out of chairs and cloth, and we enacted the royal party being greeted by the crowd. By 'freezing' and 'doubling' the action, we could find out what the members of the royal party and the crowd were thinking at the event.

For young people who may be suffering from low self-esteem or feelings of helplessness, the chance to be a king or queen, to make the rules they want and to see them enacted can be a step towards greater self-awareness. Sometimes people criticise this sort of work as 'rewarding the ones who misbehave', providing them with a 'treat'. As anyone who has participated in a therapeutic group will know, the result of a lot of hard work is that people start to address their behaviours within the group process.

Ye Min (Total Learning Challenge)

I just want to ask ...

Surely we should put our energies into therapeutic group work for the really troubled children, rather than bothering with circle time and whatever else for children who don't show any sign of being in emotional difficulties?

We consider all forms of group work to be as important as each other. Therapeutic work with troubled children helps them to engage with their peers, while the work with the whole class ensures that there is a positive emotional environment for everyone. This helps to sustain the benefits that individuals have achieved in their more intense small-group sessions at the same time as it hopefully prevents other children from getting into deeper difficulties. The overall effect is to create an atmosphere that improves the quality of learning and collaboration for everybody.

See Appendix 5 for organisations that provide therapeutic group work or relevant training.

Teaching the curriculum through dialogue

Placing dialogue at the centre of classroom life puts young people in a position where they can share insights, reflect together, work through disagreements and stimulate each other. It helps them to take responsibility for their learning, which becomes an experience of active engagement between students, as well as between students and their teachers.

Case study 13 describes how an American primary teacher, Lara Hansen, responded to the realisation that some of her students did not enjoy learning for its own sake. She linked this to the intense competitiveness that was leading them to mock each other rather than provide support. When she introduced cooperative learning activities into her reading classes, the consequence was an evident improvement in motivation. The activity that energised students most, as it happens, involved playing the role of 'teacher' to their peers.

Group work activities like these engage young people in learning as a social experience. They explore a particular subject at the same time as they are learning about each other – what strengths and weaknesses each brings to the task, how they can combine these strengths in a productive way. Opportunities are created for students to become interested in each others' perspectives as part of a process of learning how to think more deeply and find ways of valuing each other.

Emotionally literate group work helps students to engage with difficulty, to tolerate higher levels of uncertainty and to take more risks in their learning. Relying on the support of each other, they can be more adventurous in searching for information and formulating ideas.

Some dismiss a focus on collaborative enquiry as a rather circuitous route to the knowledge and the skills young people are expected to acquire through their education. This reflects a limited perspective on knowledge.

It is possible to represent history as being about dates, statutes and ways of understanding the impersonal forces that shift the affairs of men (and women); science as being about the abstract principles that govern the relationships between materials, chemicals and living things; and language about sets of grammatical principles that govern the sentence structures used by different groups.

But these academic subjects are also about the ways in which human beings interact with each other. History concerns how human relationships and conflicts lead to social and economic change; learning a new language involves grasping the ways in which particular groups of people communicate with each other, and the development of scientific understanding involves people collectively shaping challenges, information and ideas in ways that take forward what we know about the physical world.

Stimulating understanding

Approaching curriculum topics with a double perspective allows students to apply what they are learning about each other to their exploration of the human dynamics inherent in what they are seeking to understand. Such an approach can help students to appreciate why nations go to war or how Einstein developed the theory of relativity. By following it, teachers can create a win-win situation whereby they stimulate enthusiasm for learning, create more harmonious classrooms and equip students with a range of collaborative skills that will serve them well in their future lives.

Brian Matthews describes in case study 14 (about the Improving Science and Emotional Development Project) how the introduction of group work activities into science lessons replicated science as a social process, increased students' interest in and understanding of science while also fostering their abilities to get on with each other.

There is a similar lesson from case study 15. Barbara McCombs describes coming into a class where the teacher moved around the classroom while his students quietly got on with the task of learning. He had asked the students at the beginning of the term how they wanted to learn. 'We can do it anyway you want,' he told them, 'as long as you learn the maths.' His response to what they said explained their ability to focus on the subject. This led to a book (McCombs 1997).

Evidence for the value of group learning

1. Learning strategies

A study by three researchers from the Institute of Education at the University of London argues that children as young as seven can conceptualise learning and are able to articulate learning strategies and the processes they use. They suggest that pupil voice is an increasingly important element in furthering our understanding of teaching and learning more generally.

Year 6 and Year 2 children were shown four statements about learning. They were then asked if they thought them true. There was an open-ended conversation lasting between 10 and 20 minutes about the best conditions for learning. Shown the four statements again, they were then asked to write down a fifth.

The seven-year-old children believed that, if they were enjoying a lesson, they learned more. If they were bored, they were liable to be easily distracted. They emphasised their need for constant access to help, preferably through one-to-one interaction with the teacher. Their views on the best conditions for learning were:

- They were interested in having clear information from the teachers.
- They wanted work presented in an exciting way.
- They liked active involvement and sharing understanding with others.

They could describe a variety of learning strategies, and some were able to articulate their own thinking processes. They maintained a broad perception of learning, to include a social and physical understanding of their environment, even while they were trying to acquire basic skills.

The 11-year-olds saw learning as their own responsibility and preferred not to be constantly controlled.

McCallum, Hargreaves and Gipps (2000)

2. Competition and collaboration

In generally competitive environments, success at academic tasks has little value for many individuals and may even be a deterrent to popularity with peers.

A survey of 375 studies concluded that a student given opportunities to learn collaboratively performed significantly better than an average student learning within a competitive or individualistic situation.

Cooperative learning resulted in more higher-level reasoning, more frequent generation of new ideas and solutions, and greater transfer of what is learned within one situation to another.

> Cooperative learning is indicated whenever the learning goals are highly important, problem solving is desired, divergent thinking or creativity is desired, quality of performance is expected, and higher-level reasoning strategies and critical thinking are needed.

Johnson and Johnson (1994)

Case study 13
How group teaching in reading lessons enhanced the motivation of primary students

In my class, some 40 minutes of each day is dedicated to guided reading. I begin this time by reading a story to my class and then turn over the remaining time for the students to read whatever they choose in Self-Selected Reading (SSR).

When I introduced cooperative learning into our two reading blocks, a great deal of time had to be given to explaining, discussing, teaching and modelling how this was to be done. During SSR, my students were given the chance to read with a partner or in groups. They were encouraged to help each other with difficult words and to tell one another about the books they were reading.

I used an assortment of cooperative learning activities. The students participated in an activity called 'Play School Groups'. This meant they played school in groups of four. One student was assigned to be the teacher and his or her job was to help the remaining three students read the story we were working on during the week. In another activity, the students were put in groups of four and each student was given the task of teaching the other students a specific reading strategy. When the students were not participating in an organised cooperative learning activity, they were simply encouraged to constantly give help to others.

Before introducing cooperative learning into our reading blocks, I took note of the behaviours that seemed to reflect a lack of motivation. After going over these notes I realised there were seven students in particular who were having a great deal of difficulty. These seven varied in reading ability: two were my lowest readers and one was my top reader. I found these students to be disruptive to others and, in discreet ways, doing anything to distract themselves from their reading. They turned pages quickly and switched books often, obviously not reading for content, comprehension or enjoyment. They were the first to express relief once a particular reading block was over.

One might think these behaviours stemmed from books at an inappropriate reading level or that the inability to read was turning them off from books and the task of reading. I was not convinced. These students could all read. Furthermore, during our two reading blocks, a variety of books were available representing diversity in level, genre and subject. These students were simply bereft of motivation.

I also perceived an air of competition in my class. My students were hesitant to help each other. They seemed to constantly look out only for themselves. I observed students laughing at their peers as wrong answers were delivered or words were stumbled over. I found that my students would not think to ask a friend for help in pronouncing, sounding out or reading a word correctly.

Once I turned the SSR block into a cooperative effort, the results were immediate. I was thrilled to witness my 20 first-grade students happily reading in groups of two, three and four. I was amazed a few days into the study when, for the first time during SSR, I looked at the clock and realised we had gone over time. What at first had seemed like a chore, was now an activity where the students were involved, engaged and motivated.

Eventually, this reading block began to be eagerly anticipated by my students. They were seeing their peers as a valuable source of help, rather than as an opportunity for competition. The seven students I mentioned earlier were no longer disrupting and distracting others, but rather reading contentedly and successfully. I realised that, for these particular students, a cooperative strategy was essential in facilitating their motivation to read.

At the beginning of this study, my students were quite abrasive with each other as they began working cooperatively. I heard conceit in the tone of their voices. I witnessed eyes being rolled in disgust. And I saw shoulders slump with humiliation. I realised that I should have spent more time stressing appropriate behaviours, reactions and feedback. This would have built a more stable foundation for addressing the issues of constructive criticism, consideration for the feelings of others and the value of praise.

There was one particular method I used in a variety of ways that was the most successful in motivating my students – the student acting as the teacher. My students took on this responsibility with interest and eagerness. It was the cooperative strategy that was requested the most, and it made a contribution to the various signs of intrinsic motivation – enthusiasm, a high attention span, persistence and a rise in self-esteem.

Lara Hansen (2001)

Case study 14

How emotional literacy can help secondary students become more interested in science

Contrary to popular opinion, science is inherently a social activity. Science incorporates imagination, creativity, and social and political values. Our education system needs to recognise this. Developing social and emotional understanding in science can bring three benefits:

- stimulating interest in, and understanding of, the nature of science;
- developing positive methods of communication that promote well-being and collaboration;
- maintaining academic success.

p.47
For pupils to progress emotionally they need to gain an understanding of each other and, in particular, to do so across gender divides. **Dialogue** and the ensuing interplay is seen as central to helping pupils develop their sense of 'self' and 'other'.

The aims of the Improving Science and Emotional Development (ISED) Project were:

- to develop pupils' communication skills in science lessons, using collaborative learning techniques with feedback;
- to develop pupils' emotional skills with each other, and especially for boys and girls to gain a greater understanding of each other.

The overall strategy was for pupils to work in mixed-sex groups, self-monitor and make written comments on their cognitive and social interactions. They then have both aspects of development on the agenda and can discuss issues, engage their emotion and so, hopefully, develop as people. Research lessons are done about once every three weeks.

The full process was as follows. Pupils work initially in groups of five, so that one can be an observer who watches and make notes while two boys and two girls work together. A task is set so that the two boys and two girls can work and talk about and learn some science for about ten to 15 minutes. A prepared sheet is given to the observer who fills it out, noting who talked and listened, if anyone was supportive and if there were frequent interruptions.

When the activity is stopped, the observer fills in totals on the sheet and makes any relevant notes on how the group worked and socialised together. While the observers are doing this, the two boys and two girls fill in a sheet in silence to indicate how they, and the others in the group, did on the same criteria as the observer used. The pupils are then given time to discuss their views. In fact, time for this has been short and sometimes missed. These discussions have then gone on informally, which is probably the best place for them.

Once the pupils are familiar with the procedures, the observer is not used and pupils work in groups of four. They then fill in sheets that ask a variety of questions about social and cognitive skills. Here is a selection from the six different sheets:

- Who do you think suggested useful things to do?
- How well did you get on with the rest of your group?
- Were there any differences with sex or race?
- Does group work affect how you feel about science?

The above procedures are done with collaborative learning exercises, and also alongside normal teaching, for example, during practical work or completing a worksheet. The procedures are designed to legitimate pupil-pupil and pupil-teacher discussions around social and emotional issues as well as cognitive ones. In essence, we are trying to get pupils to develop a social coherence based on accepting each other and their differences. They need to value each other for those differences.

A special database was developed to analyse the responses from students for any patterns in their responses, and to look at how accurately pupils predicted the extent to which they talked and listened. Overall the pattern of talking, while varying considerably from group to group and with time, indicates a good balance between contributions from both boys and girls with, if anything, girls saying slightly more.

The pupils are generally keen on the research. They have indicated clearly that as this sort of work continues so they gain a greater understanding of each other. Also, as one would expect, they often do not find it easy to work together, but realise how important it is that they develop the necessary skills. One girl said of working with boys 'Sometimes they're silly, but once we shout at them they're quite alright.'

In a questionnaire given at the beginning and end of the year the pupils of both sexes reported that they would be happier working with each other, and that they looked forward to it more. Here are some illustrative quotes:

'Sometimes it [group work in science] makes you get on better with people but sometimes they disagree but I think that is good for girls to work with boys and boys to work with girls because it will probably help you to understand the other sex and race' (girl).

'You get to know people who I never worked with [until we did group work]' (boy).

'Very important because other people's views matter just as much as yours' (girl).

The boys and girls also said that at the end of the year they were keener to work in groups rather than by themselves, and that their preference for mixed-sex groups had also increased, although these were small changes.

The boys and girls also indicated that they believed that they had improved their inter-gender interpersonal skills. For example, they felt much more confident of saying what they wanted to people of the other sex. They also said that they understood the other sex much better. They also understood the same sex a bit better.

There was also an increase in their feeling that the other sex would like them and that the other sex would help them learn. Here are some quotes from interviews:

> *Kamila*: Science is enjoyable and it's fun when you work with people in groups, you socialise a lot.

> *Steven*: It's good because then you can see that if one of you is not good at science and one of you is then if you work together you get better.

> *Jim*: Yeah, and also you get different opinions and different ideas for science and what we're doing. And if someone gets stuck you can help them out … and they can help you out.

The teachers have found that doing this research work helps in many ways. They are getting to know the children better, give them a wider range of classroom activities than normal and the classroom atmosphere is improved. The approach leads to less work in that it gives more time in the classroom to listen and so to get to know the pupils better.

Here is a quote from a teacher:

> If they are more confident they think better about themselves, they are not scared to go and do things, they don't think, 'Oh, I can't do that because I am not as good as them.' They are willing to have a try because they've got the confidence that nobody in the class will laugh at them and make fun of them if they get it wrong. They won't get into trouble, and that sort of thing, so their whole self-esteem improves.

Many questions arise out of this type of research. The following gives a flavour of the issues:

- Certain pupils do not get on with everyone. Should we mix them up more or less?
- Boys often say that they get more work done when working with girls. So do they gain academically?
- Girls often say that boys do not get on with the work. Yet they say they like the humour they bring. What are the implications of this?
- Girls say that other girls can be catty, whereas boys are not. So is it possible that girls can gain socially from this work?
- Is this not the reverse to what is normally believed, which is that boys can gain socially from the 'civilising' influence of girls? Can both statements be true?
- This study is taking place in science lessons where gender boundaries tend to be comparatively strictly drawn. What would happen if the same approach was used in other subjects?
- How much should we put pupils together to enable them to learn socially and emotionally?

This research is producing strong evidence that this sort of work can contribute to the social and emotional development of pupils. We are certain that there is a potential for progress, and it is being developed by the approaches of the research. We hope that by encouraging dialogue, pupils are then coming to understand the complexity of the 'other' and so are helped to understand their inner selves more.

Brian Matthews (2001)
pea01bm@gold.ac.uk

Case study 15

Students from a gang-infested community become absorbed by mathematics

A middle school in Aurora, Colorado, was working on a project entitled 'Neighbors Making a Difference' which was aimed at fostering positive relationships between teachers and their students (as well as between students and other meaningful adults in their immediate community). It was part of a strategy for offsetting student gang involvement and drug use.

Many of the teachers at this middle school had expressed fear of these 'tough' students. They said that there was little they could do to reach them. I decided to spend a day at the school so that I could see what was happening in the classrooms. This involved sitting unobtrusively at the back of the class, following a group of students throughout their class periods in order to get a closer look at the dynamics in the relationships between the ill-reputed students and their struggling teachers.

After the experience, I somewhat wryly remarked to someone that I was 'amazed the students weren't schizophrenic'. Explaining, I related how observing a variety of different classes throughout the day was like an 'up and down rollercoaster', with students in some classes behaving in stark opposition to the students in others. I witnessed several teachers desperately trying to control their students in rowdy and unruly classroom settings.

To top it off, I was witness to a student fight in the hallways right before a final period maths class. Apparently, this was not an atypical experience for these middle school pupils. I could not help but wonder to what length such students would go to disrupt the traditionally unpopular subject of maths, particularly positioned at the end of a long school day.

To my surprise, however, I was privy to a quite surreal yet inspiring display. The students filed into the class, and I waited expectantly for all hell to break loose. Without the prominent presence of a teacher, the students immediately became quiet and self-disciplined, picking out the appropriate materials from folders positioned along the side of the classroom. They sat down at their desks, paired up into preset groups to work on their current computer projects and promptly began to work without even the slightest command or provocation from a teacher.

I finally noticed the teacher standing in the back of the room. Realising that he was not a domineering, rote, 'stand and deliver' type of teacher, I watched how he interacted with the students in the class. What I saw was that he periodically walked around and checked student work already in progress. Clearly, there was much to be learned from this teacher and his seemingly effortless style in facilitating a self-directed learning process for the students.

Here was a teacher who trusted students to regulate and motivate themselves. And that is what was happening. Not only was the teacher freed from keeping his students in control, he also was able to support and engage them in meaningful assignments. The result was positive motivation bereft of any student disturbances or complaints.

After the maths class was over, I could not resist asking the teacher how he had achieved such an impressive feat. He explained his philosophy about students' natural desire to learn and the events that led to his successful classroom environment. At the beginning of the year, the teacher said, he simply and directly told the students that: 'This is your class. We can do it anyway you want as long you learn the maths.' In other words, while the teacher did lay out his 'non-negotiables' – the essential elements necessary to cover content standards and to ensure that the work got done – he largely left the overall options and details up to his students.

Apparently, in leaving many of the choices and the rules for managing the class up to his students, the teacher had gained their respect. He relayed that not only were students harder on themselves in setting up classroom rules than he would have been, but they also felt ownership and enforced the rules. His job was easier and he had helped instil in the students a sense of responsibility and motivation that transcended everything except their desire to learn.

Dr Barbara McCombs
bmccombs@du.edu

I just want to ask ...

How do we ensure that time spent on emotional literacy saves time currently spent on less productive activity – like trying to impose order in the classroom or fulfilling unnecessary bureaucratic requirements?

Emotional literacy is a strategy for rebuilding trust in our schools so that there is less micro-management, better systems for sharing with each other our teaching and learning strategies. For example, an emotionally literate approach to lesson planning might make more time for teaching with collegial observation. This would reduce the need for individual teachers to submit detailed lesson plans, while at the same time ensuring that the best ideas and methods were shared.

See Appendix 6 for organisations with an interest in emotionally literate ways of working.

School democracy

The establishment of citizenship as a central element in both the primary and the secondary curriculum – with its emphasis on fostering the skills of enquiry and communication, participation and responsible action – has encouraged the growth of interest in schools councils, class councils and other forms of democratic activity within schools.

These initiatives can foster emotional understanding if they acknowledge that the best way to ensure students act responsibly is to give them responsibility; that those who feel able to influence the organisations in which their lives are embedded are much more likely to experience well-being; and that it is students who know best what are the factors in the way their school is run that block or have the potential to facilitate their capacity to learn.

In case study 17, Michael Fielding describes the experience of a group of secondary students who were invited to carry out an action research project on sex education. As a result, they increased their awareness of why some teachers were not good at handling this area of PSHE – they were too embarrassed – and used this understanding to evolve a strategy that involved engaging older students in teaching.

A commitment to valuing student voice, and giving young people the opportunity to work out ways of making things work better, tends to generate high levels of collective energy as new ideas and solutions are generated. Like the students at Sharnbrook Upper, the primary pupil in case study 16 who took part in a project at Wheatcroft Primary School talks about the excitement he and others experienced at having the opportunity to make a real difference to the way in which the school was run.

These processes have an enormous potential to contribute to the growth of emotional literacy within a school. Their capacity to do this depends largely on whether they are supported by the sort of relationship building described in the rest of this book, and whether there is a real commitment on the part of management to letting students speak about what truly concerns them.

The challenge for school leaders is to accept the risks involved in opening up channels of communication, and then to tolerate whatever emerges from the process. Ann Burgess and Neil Spencelayh, whose experiment in **leadership** is p.87 described in case study 18, recall how the happiness they felt when a teacher raised the funds for a community arts project turned to horror when they saw the result – a larger-than-life-sized statue of the school caretaker with an aggressive stance, and a display of J-cloths, pan scrubs and plastic gloves in the school entrance. They struggled to overcome a first instinct to remove these eyesores, realising it was important to value the fact that a member of staff and a group of children had made something happen.

Like political issues in the wider world, school politics stir powerful emotions. Different emotional agendas bubble behind people's views and arguments on specific topics. Over particular issues, students and teachers may find themselves experiencing rage, hope or some sort of feeling in between. These responses reflect their personal histories and the nature of what they hope for and are afraid of.

By managing these democratic processes to bring these emotional responses out into the open so that they can be talked about and examined, a discourse can emerge that gets to the heart of what is really going on, and enables decisions about the management of the school and its curriculum to take more fully into account the emotional consequences that will flow from them. In open and emotionally literate dialogue lies the opportunity to bring together the school's collective understanding and imagination to shape a more dynamic learning community.

Case study 16

Student voice at Wheatcroft Primary School

My name is Oliver and I am in Year 6. Recently, we have become involved in a research project that is looking at pupil voice. The improvements this research has made for our school have been amazing.

Here are some of the projects we have developed using pupil voice. Some pupils said that they get hungry during lessons, so we started a tuck shop during break-time. Since then, no more hunger complaints have been made.

Some pupils said that the playground was getting a bit boring, so we had a playground day where, instead of lessons, we worked outside on improving our playground. Some of our new features include a bug world, which will help with our science. Camps, which we built out of wood, will help with our design and technology. Most importantly, we had fun.

Using pupil voice, we are managing to work, have fun and, if necessary, to complain. Some pupils in my class believe that just sitting in front of a board may help you to work but, without fun, learning is not interesting. Therefore, children can lose interest in working.

I think that a lot of schools would benefit from listening to pupil voice. That way, pupils feel better by knowing that teachers will listen to them. I know that almost everybody in our school does.

Oliver, pupil at Wheatcroft School (2001)

Case study 17

How giving students a genuine voice in the running of the school can transform relationships and learning

What came to be known as the Students as Researchers Project began life in November 1996 as part of Sharnbrook Upper School's participation in the Improving the Quality of Education for All school improvement initiative based at the University of Cambridge School of Education.

As part of a concerted effort to involve students more substantially in the life of the school, a group of students of mixed age and gender and a range of attainment was brought together and trained in research and evidence-gathering techniques. The aim was for students themselves to identify issues they saw as important in their daily experience of schooling and, with the support of three staff acting as facilitators, to gather data, make meaning together and put forward recommendations for change. As such it was a quantum leap, not only from traditional approaches to student involvement such as student councils and peer-led learning, but also from the engagement of students in staff-led action research. Here the location of power, perspective and energising dynamic was to rest primarily in the collective control of the students themselves.

The first cohort consisted of 15 students ranging from Year 9 (aged 13 years) to Year 13 (aged 17 years). The group decided to explore three topics: student voice, student experience of trainee teachers, and the school's assessment and profiling system. Over the next two months subgroups gathered data on each topic, then produced reports setting out their research intentions, outlining their methodology, presenting their data and its analysis, and offering recommendations for future action. Student researchers presented their reports at parents' evenings, governing body meetings, student council meetings, tutor groups, staff meetings and also to special interest groups in each research area.

In two of the research areas the work had substantial and immediate impact: the school's assessment and profiling system has changed in ways that explicitly acknowledge the students' recommendations, and members of the school council are now entitled to a range of training and support which acknowledges the demanding nature of their role. The recommendations regarding students' experience of trainee teachers encountered initial resistance within the teacher training institutions. Two years later, however, six trainee teachers and 22 students joined a pilot scheme to explore their respective and mutual experience of teaching and learning.

The second year involved a slightly larger cohort of students, including some experienced student researchers acting as student consultants, i.e. in an advisory capacity. Again three research groups emerged, looking this time at aspects of careers education, the quality of school meals and the life skills programme. The data gathering became more sophisticated, more varied and more imaginative. The impact of all three groups was visible and significant, but the most far-reaching recommendations came from the life skills group.

The life skills group queried the school policy which insisted that all tutors deliver a programme including issues like adolescent sexuality and drugs education, which many staff felt ill-equipped to teach. Students felt embarrassed on teachers' behalf and suggested greater involvement of external or highly motivated and trained people at particular points, including older students in the school. They also highlighted the limitations of overly didactic methods which gave them little scope to use IT skills or to engage in more active forms of learning. Most radically, they argued for a move away from a predetermined curriculum to a negotiated programme that acknowledged students' own perspectives and concerns. As a result of this student research, the school substantially revised the life skills programme and, even more radically, recruited three students to the group monitoring and evaluating the new provision.

What we are witnessing here are profound cultural and structural changes in the professional identity and working practices of a large, very successful secondary comprehensive school, changes that are student-led and sustained by the richness and attentiveness of a dialogic culture.

Students as Researchers valorises and extends a transformative model of education at the heart of which lies the commitment to teaching and learning as a genuinely shared responsibility. Five years on, the school has nearly 90 student researchers and 14 staff working together in curriculum teams. Student voice has moved from the periphery of organisational maintenance to the centre of curriculum renewal.

Michael Fielding (2001)

The student's point of view

In the early years of my school life, my education was something I was only a part of and I had no reason to question anything that was done to me. In my lower and middle schools I had been socialised to accept what I had and not search for something else because that something was not there.

When I entered the first year of upper school, I carried on as usual just having education done to me and not responding to anything other than what was inside the classroom. At the end of my first year at upper school I had my end-of-year interview with my form tutor who told me I was not an active participant within the school community and that I needed to get more involved.

In February 1996 (the spring term of Year 10), I was approached by the deputy head teacher of the school and asked to become involved in the Students as Researchers project. After talking to some friends, I decided to accept the offer.

I was trained in research methods and the ethics of research and formed with a group that was to be looking at profiling and assessment within the school. We spent approximately six months gathering data and preparing findings ready to feed into the senior management team of the school. At the time the teachers in the school were looking at the same topic as us, so at times we worked together and from the combined research, profiling and assessment changed within the school.

This was my motivation to keep going. Finally I had found that extra niche that I needed in order to keep me interested in my studies and motivate me to come to school. Some work I had done had influenced the school's feelings about profiling – so much so that they had changed it. That gave me a great sense of achievement.

Over the four years that I did the project I looked at a number of things that would make an impact on the school. I have given presentations to both small and large numbers of staff and students. I have worked with all school years, which no other aspect of school life would have allowed me to do. I learned how to coordinate a small group of people, how to keep them on task and motivated. These are all things that will stay with me for the rest of my life and are all part of the bigger picture of education.

I have learned so much from Students as Researchers, yet I had to make it take a back seat to my studies when exam pressures arose. I understand that qualifications are important but so are other educational needs. For me, this was an educational need and I was lucky enough to be given the opportunity to do it. I would not have seen my A levels through, had I not been part of it. Others may have dropped out of school because of the lack of student voice within the school community. Education is not something that should be done to you, but something you should be part of.

Christopher Harding (2001)

I just want to ask ...

How do we acknowledge our differences and negotiate a way through them, rather than creating a phoney consensus?

We are so accustomed to the idea that the best way to resolve any issue is by polarising it that we find it hard to imagine how looking for ways of agreeing can end up in anything other than a messy fudge. What the polarising tendency does is to put all the emphasis on the area of disagreement. An emotionally literate approach seeks to map out the areas of agreement more fully, and also to explore what lies behind the solid nuggets of disagreement that remain. Often what we find is that there is a common anxiety explaining the disagreement which leads the parties in different directions. Identifying that often helps them come up with something that suits them both.

Evidence for the value of school democracy

Derry Hannam looked at schools that were taking the participation and responsible action elements of the Citizenship Order seriously for significant numbers of students through the full range of academic ability. He set out to test the hypothesis that, in such schools, an improvement in attainment would be found across the full range of GCSE results, though not necessarily mainly at the higher grades.

The underlying belief was that, if the hypothesis proved to be correct, it would be because participation promoted higher self-esteem and a greater sense of owner-ship and empowerment of students, leading to greater motivation to 'engage' with learning across the curriculum.

The definition of student participation developed was:

Learning to collaborate with others (peers and/or adults) in the identification of needs, tasks, problems within the school or wider community, to ask appropriate questions and gather appropriate information, to discuss and negotiate possible courses of action, to share in planning and decision making, to share the responsibility for implementing the plan, to evaluate, review and reflect upon outcomes and to communicate these to others.

Twelve schools were identified as meeting the high participation criteria. The overwhelming view of senior managers was that participation impacted benefi-cially on self-esteem, motivation, sense of ownership and empowerment, which in turn enhances attainment.

The overwhelming view of the students interviewed was that the participative activities were of great benefit to them in a variety of ways. They require students to take initiatives and decisions. This generates motivation, ownership and a sense of being independent, trusted and responsible. This supports the learning of com-munication and collaboration skills. These facilitate 'quality' outcomes that both intrinsically and through recognition from others lead to enhanced self-esteem. Out of this comes an overall sense of personal and social 'efficacy'.

Involvement in student participative activities brought real benefits to relation-ships between students and teachers. There was anecdotal evidence that this led to enhanced attainment.

Students believed that involvement in participative activities enhanced learning across the curriculum – sometimes in unexpected and unpredictable ways. In many cases, students described the development of important organisational and time-management skills in order to ensure that the participatory activities had no adverse effect on their 'regular' school work. Students who were missing all or part of lessons as a result of participatory activities spoke of developing greater powers of concentration in order to squeeze the maximum benefit from the time when they were in lessons.

Hannam (2001)

See Appendix 7 for organisations promoting democracy, citizenship and values education.

4

Strategies

The qualities of an emotionally literate school

An emotionally literate school works to realise six core values.

Safety

There is a commitment to providing sufficient emotional security to enable people to engage with what they are feeling, so that people say:

I can trust that what people say to me is what they mean and that there is not a hidden agenda – Transparency

It feels like we are all working together for a common purpose – Cohesion

I believe other people will respond to me in a way that is supportive – Trust

Openness

There is a commitment to openness and honesty in all areas of school life, so that people say:

The information I need is available to me in a form that I can understand and use – Accessibility

This organisation places importance on the alignment of the personal and professional – Alignment

I am able to share my feelings and experiences openly with those I work with – Openness

Compassion

There is a commitment to taking a genuine interest in the experience of others and supporting them to become who they are, so that people say:

The information I receive expresses affection and genuine interest – Warmth

This organisation supports me personally as well as professionally – Support

I sense that people have a commitment to understanding my feelings and experiences – Empathy

Connection

There is a commitment to bringing people together so that they may know and learn from each other, so that people say:

Communication within this organisation enables me to feel closer to others – Engagement

This organisation encourages people to learn from and with each other – Collaboration

I feel connected to others in a way that enables me to feel part of a team – Relatedness

Reflection

There is a commitment to taking the time to deepen people's understanding of each other and of what is happening in the organisation, so that people say:

Communication is characterised by mutual listening and response – Dialogic

The organisation recognises the need for us to explore together the implications of any action being proposed that is going to significantly affect us – Reflection-orientation

People appreciate the unique contribution I make to this organisation – Respect

Growth-orientation

There is a commitment to actively enabling everybody to achieve their potential and to flourish, so that people say:

Communication here develops our capacity to engage more of ourselves in our lives and work – Development

This organisation encourages people to believe in their own potential and creativity and expects that they will achieve it – Empowerment

I feel that other people in this organisation value me as a person – Value

	Safety	Openness	Compassion	Connection	Reflection	Growth-orientation
Communication	Transparency	Accessibility	Warmth	Engagement	Dialogue	Development
Organisation	Cohesion	Alignment	Support	Collaboration	Reflection-orientation	Empowerment
Relationship	Trust	Openness	Empathy	Relatedness	Respect	Value

The Matrix of Emotional Literacy represents the elements identified through Antidote's Emotional Literacy Audit, which has been developed by Alice Haddon.

Matrix of emotional literacy

Strategies for sustainability

Everyone in and around a school community has a responsibility for its emotional literacy. The government official shaping a letter to head teachers, a parent deciding how to engage with her child's school or a head teacher planning the way she will run a staff meeting, each model an attitude that will reverberate through the school, shaping the ways in which people relate to each other.

Emotional literacy and illiteracy are contagious. The government minister who feels stressed by the pressure he is under to deliver targets is more likely to badger head teachers than one who is offered a way to cope; the head teacher who is frustrated at being required to do things he does not believe in will be less attentive to students than one who feels able to transform the latest directive into something he can work with; the young person who feels that school management does not treat him with respect is more likely to take his rage out on a fellow student.

If a school is to practise emotional literacy, all its stakeholders must take some responsibility for trying to understand the emotions that drive them and to generate emotional understanding.

People often ask what works in promoting emotional literacy. The answer we give is that everything works and nothing works. It is not what people do that matters, but how they do it. There is no point in giving young people opportunities to speak in a circle unless the messages they receive from their teachers and other staff are that it is all right to speak about the things that matter to them, that there will be a meaningful response to what emerges and that they are ready to be surprised by what they hear.

The challenge of developing an effective emotional literacy strategy is to increase the probability that every interaction in a school will facilitate the development of emotional understanding. Whether a teacher is talking to someone in a corridor, designing a physics lesson or running a circle time with the whole class, emotional literacy will grow if each of these occasions can be used as opportunities for people to deepen their emotional understanding.

Getting started

Members of a school community who want to raise levels of emotional literacy need to ask themselves three questions: What elements in your life in this school block your capacity to practise emotional literacy? What elements facilitate it? Where are the opportunities for improvement?

By using a process such as Antidote's Emotional Literacy Audit (ELA) to gather together, and reflect on, the many different answers that people provide to these questions, staff and students can evolve a range of more specific questions. How, for example, can we structure our staff meetings in a way that enables us to communicate what really matters to us? How can space in the school be better used to encourage people to share ideas and discover a sense of belonging? And how can different activities be integrated so that they have a mutually beneficial impact on each other? The issues identified are likely to indicate the most strategic points for intervention.

The open exploration of these questions generates fresh ideas for tackling them. Could we use circle time in a different way to address that issue? Might there be a way of opening up that issue in the school council? How about bringing together a group of staff to examine ways of meeting that challenge? Should we arrange for someone to come and train us up in that approach?

By following these questions and engaging in a reflective discussion upon them, staff and students can begin to evolve ideas that are informed by what the organisation knows about itself, that value the insights of the people who know the organisation from the inside, that stimulate their creativity and have the potential to carry conviction among the people who have to implement them.

There are ten principles to bear in mind when shaping an emotional literacy strategy:

- Emotional literacy is a process rather than a goal.
- Emotional literacy is about releasing our capacity to learn with and from each other.
- Emotional literacy is generated through dialogue.
- Dialogue cannot happen without reflection.
- Dialogue enables us to develop new stories about ourselves as learners.
- Emotional literacy is sustained through our continuing curiosity.
- Small changes across a whole organisation will have a bigger impact than a big change in one part of an organisation.
- Adults need the same opportunities as young people to practise emotional literacy.
- Every interaction is an opportunity to facilitate or inhibit emotional literacy.
- Every organisation has untapped resources for promoting emotional literacy.

If a school is to become and remain truly responsive to the changing needs of its staff and students, it needs to keep on asking what is going on. How are changes in the wider community affecting the emotional climate of the school? Which of the school's structures and processes are working well to promote emotional literacy and which need to be refined or rethought?

The process of asking these questions, reflecting on what the answers say about how the emotional climate might be improved and then generating activities that will bring this about, is a continuous cycle.

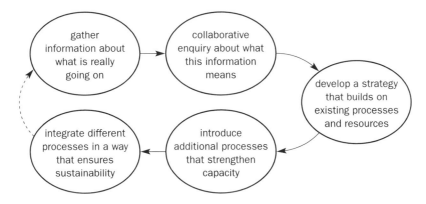

The emotional literacy development cycle

Leaders

If emotional literacy is to flourish in a school, its staff, students and parents need to know that they can influence the actions and decisions that are being taken to improve the quality of teaching and learning within the school.

For this to happen, senior managers need to be genuinely interested in what other people are thinking and saying, and to be capable of integrating the many different voices present in the school so as to demonstrate that they truly have been heard. It is important that they show they are capable of doing something with whatever is presented to them, and that there is a possibility they will themselves be transformed by what they have heard, seen or felt.

It helps if they can be always curious about what is, or might be, going on; can actively promote processes that enable staff and students to explore together the questions they have about how the school should be managed, how improvements in behaviour and academic achievement can be brought about, how the goals of the organisation need to be revised or whatever else.

Useful reading

Sharp, P. (2001) *Nurturing Emotional Literacy: A practical guide for teachers, parents and those in the caring professions*. London: David Fulton Publishers.

Sharp sets out a practical approach to developing the capacity to 'recognise, understand, handle and appropriately express emotions'. He is very clear that this is not just another lesson for young people: 'nurturing emotional literacy,' as he says, 'begins with you.' Whether we are teachers, parents, carers or service managers, we cannot expect to help young people develop emotional and social competence unless we have nurtured such competence in ourselves. Personal development gives rise to a commitment on the group and organisational level. The book contains chapters for teachers, learners, parents, carers and local authorities, each ending with an 'action' box suggesting practical ways of moving towards an emotionally literate education system and society. Sharp concludes with a discussion of the emotional literacy initiative in Southampton and the potential of emotional literacy to impact fundamentally and positively upon health, the economy, the workplace, government, leisure and the criminal justice system.

Weare, K. (2000) *Promoting Mental, Emotional and Social Health: A Whole School Approach*. London: Routledge.

Weare explores the evidence for the importance of social and emotional education, and the principles and practices whose application can improve morale and well-being, while also raising academic attainment. She sets out a process for implementing change, starting with a review of where people are starting from. Using that information, schools can design a learning programme that builds up in small steps, deploying a wide range of methods of teaching and learning, and involving pupils and teachers in designing their own programmes. Weare ends with a section on the importance of teacher education, citing research to demonstrate that when teachers are supported in improving their own emotional and social skills, there is a dramatic improvement in pupils' learning and behaviour, and in teachers' own sense of fulfilment.

Weare, K. (2003) *Developing the Emotionally Literate School*. London: Sage.

This book explores the relevance of new research on whole-brain development and learning styles. It also has sections on the profiling and assessment of emotional literacy, as well as on how LEAs can provide effective support for this work in schools. The heart of Weare's argument is that the only really effective way to promote emotional literacy is through a whole-school approach. It is the school environment that most powerfully influences the capacity of young people (and their teachers) to feel good about themselves, to engage with each other, to make a positive contribution to the school community and to get on with the business of studying.

The aim is to create an environment in which others can take the initiative; to ensure that people experience collaborative relationships that engender good thinking and creative ideas. This is more likely to happen if senior managers are continuously trying to move the power to effect change out into the wider school community, allowing for the possibility of ideas coming from anyone who sees opportunities for doing something better or differently.

At the same time, they need to manage and process the pressures that come from outside the school. That means demonstrating their own capacity to think when pressures are bearing down upon them, and to transform their own angry or anxious emotions into productive energy, without at the same time denying their feelings. They need to keep people's focus on the goals being pursued rather than the means being proposed to achieve them, to stimulate people's desire for change and their belief that it can be achieved.

In case study 18, the head and deputy of Hartsholme Primary School describe how they were able to engender a quality of conversation that allowed the situation of the school to be seen in a broad perspective, and to generate responses that were creative and appropriate. The anxieties created by the situation might have led to rigid and formal responses. However, the quality of the dialogue was such that ideas which initially appeared 'wild' and 'unformed' became instead the seedbed for successful practice.

Leaders achieve this ability to balance firmness and responsiveness through the conversations they hold with each other, and with other members of the school community. They learn in their interactions with others about what is happening, what needs to change, what people are asking for. By continuously seeking to learn more about themselves, about others and about the best way to accomplish the current task, they encourage their colleagues to do the same.

Case study 18

How two primary school leaders started modelling a different sort of relationship with each other and transformed the culture of their school

When Hartsholme Primary School was inspected in May 2001, the inspectors found no whole-school strengths and significant weaknesses in leadership and management at all levels, as well as in the quality of teaching and learning. It was not a promising prospect for Neil who arrived as the deputy head in September or for Ann who was seconded in the following month as the fourth acting head in rapid succession. But over seven months, their unplanned partnership succeeded in moving the school forward through the quality of the dialogue they created between them. The following is their account of what happened.

We knew we had to do something radical but had no idea what, nor did we set out to formulate a strategy. The post-Ofsted action plan set out actions to address the issues but did not tackle the culture that would underpin the actions. It was fortunate that we worked well together from the start and that the relationship developed into an increasingly effective one. We acted instinctively in accordance with what we believed to be important about education. Our philosophies, while not the same, were compatible. Our experience and skills were complementary.

The way in which the dialogue developed between us took us by surprise, both by its immediate success and its impact. We talked, every day and all the time. In order to make sense of what we saw and what we were trying to do, we sometimes started off with quite wild or unformed ideas, or started discussions making no sense whatsoever. By articulating our thoughts, questioning and supporting each other, we developed strategies for making our ideas into practical possibilities.

Conventional wisdom says that discussions around school improvement must be tightly focused and kept 'on track' to avoid wasting time. We probably had our best ideas 'off track', often from a random thought being seemingly plucked out of the air. There were instances in our ramblings when one of us would start to tell a story or relate an experience and say, 'I'm not sure why I'm saying this' or 'I'm not sure what the significance of it is', and then the other person would be able to pick up and suggest what the connection might be.

Far from wasting time, this helped to bring about rapid improvement. There was an unspoken understanding that anything could be voiced. Nothing was taboo, nothing unmentionable. The expression of a thought or idea, however ludicrous it sounded, triggered a train of thought that could be formed into a workable solution of a kind that we would never have predicted. If we had waited for one of us to have a sensible or fully formed idea, we would not have moved forward so quickly. Had we been thinking or working individually, many ideas would never have survived the original thought, but would have been dismissed as 'ridiculous'. Ideas, once articulated, became 'real', and we began to see possibilities we could never otherwise have envisaged.

Another significant feature was the philosophical nature of the dialogue. To an outsider, it might have seemed strange for leaders of a school in special measures to be talking about philosophy rather than action. We felt that frantic activity would not help us unless we could establish what we believed and instinctively felt about education in this place. Our conversations were much more about 'I wonder' or 'What would happen if?' than they were about 'What should we do?' It was about extending the range of possibilities, pushing our imagination as far as it could go. No idea was too outrageous to consider.

The dialogue 'cemented' our professional partnership. We got to know each other and each other's values. We discovered that we both wanted a school culture where everyone collectively owned the process of education and school development. It also provided a model of cooperation and teamwork for the rest of the school.

The dialogue was bound up with the joint leadership style we developed, and also with the ethos we were trying to create. We had inherited a school where the staff and pupils felt that others came in and did things to them. It was a school where people were left to sink or swim. There were few whole-school strategies, nor was there any sense of a common cause. We knew that the key to altering this culture was successfully drawing other staff into dialogical working.

Individually we were good at our jobs; together we created between us what has been described as 'an energy that is tangible, like a third person'. Our professional and personal trust in each other helped to extend our leadership far beyond what we thought possible.

It was the quality of the dialogue we had with each other that enabled us to start distributing the process through the rest of the school. We carried out professional interviews together which created a 'trialogue' with staff. Because we did not stand on ceremony with each other, the staff learned not to stand on ceremony with us.

Although we had presented staff with opportunities to engage in dialogue themselves, it did not happen. So we modelled a professional dialogue for the whole staff and then introduced a model for them to develop an aspect of their practice through dialogue with a colleague. This activity not only helped disperse dialogue, it also 'opened up' the leadership to scrutiny, and staff appreciated that we had taken a risk in exposing our interactions to them. As well, it raised their consciousness of how things could be done differently.

Neil Spencelayh and Ann Burgess

I just want to ask ...

How do we learn to trust that others with different levels of experience and power – be they students, parents, junior staff or managers – will join in dialogue with us and understand our point of view?

Precisely by recognising that we are all in the same emotional boat. It can be hard for those lower down a hierarchy not to feel that they are powerless, or to become surly in the presence of those who have more power. At the same time, it is difficult for those further up the hierarchy not to take the occasional act of defiance or disaffection as an indication of an obtuse resistance to change that has to be met with firmness. If both parties can acknowledge how they are driven by the anxieties associated with their respective positions, they can start working together to achieve a mutual shift in the direction of each other.

Teachers and other school staff

Jennifer Nias has written;

> Teachers are emotionally committed to many different aspects of their jobs. This is not an indulgence; it is a professional necessity. Without feeling, without the freedom to 'face themselves', to be whole persons in the classroom, they implode, explode – or walk away.
>
> **Nias (1996)**

The approach described in this book asks of teachers and other staff that they find ways to remain emotionally present with their students, trying always to listen well so that they can respond well. It is in the way they reply to questions and engage with conflicts, how far they communicate to young people that they are respected, understood and valued, that they will have their most powerful impact on students' ability to practise emotional literacy.

There is solid evidence to support the claim that these qualities encourage young people to learn. When training consultancy Hay McBer (2000) was commissioned by the Department for Education and Employment (as it then was) to investigate the skills that underpinned teacher effectiveness, they concluded that, among other things, effective teachers had strengths in understanding others, in influencing people to perform and in promoting teamwork. They understood what motivated people and what blocked their learning. They not only provided help and support to colleagues, but they sought and valued their ideas.

All of this is, however, a lot to ask of staff who are under heavy pressure to deliver the curriculum, achieve higher standards and deal with the consequences of pressing social problems. The urgency of the tasks they are being required to accomplish can seem to leave little room for equally important tasks, such as finding out what is going on for their students, appreciating the way they are learning and thinking, paying attention to the feelings that are floating around the room, the corridor or the playground.

Contrasting approaches to leadership

Promoting emotional literacy

The experience and perspectives of participants in the dialogue provide the starting point for any discussion.

The group owns the principles of its operation while looking outside itself for guidelines about good practice.

Leaders identify and articulate the parameters within which the group operates.

The organisation recognises itself as being more than the sum of its members.

The group's ideas and decisions differ from those that might have been defined by any individual or subgroup.

The group collectively owns its ideas and decisions.

Leaders question the group about what it is doing and how it can be enabled to do better.

The ends of the dialogic process cannot be specified in advance and the outcomes are therefore unpredictable.

People have a commitment to dialogue in their work together.

Leaders tend to be invisible as participants in the group.

Leaders view group members as people with potential that they need to recognise, use and develop.

Leaders talk about 'us' and 'we'.

Blocking emotional literacy

The impetus to discussion comes from organisational imperatives.

The group has its practices imposed from outside or from what has traditionally been the case.

Leaders transmit and articulate non-negotiable parameters that they have defined.

The organisation is made up of people seeking to protect their individual positions.

The group's decisions either represent the lowest common denominator or the views of a controlling person or subgroup.

Individuals and subgroups can veto what they do not want and opt out.

Leaders are there to tell the group how it ought to act.

The aims of the process are imposed and non-negotiable.

Authority is used to curtail discussion and dialogue is dismissed as time-wasting, threatening or likely to generate conflict.

Leaders are highly visible even if they pay passing tribute to their teams.

Leaders view group members as people who need to already have their optimum potential available.

Leaders talk about 'them', 'my team' and 'my people'.

This chart is based on ideas coming out of a dialogue between Geoffrey Court, Harriet Goodman, Ann Burgess and Neil Burgess.

The capacity of staff to rise to this challenge will be affected by the quality of the conversations they are able to have together. Does the culture encourage them to share difficulties and learn from each other? Are opportunities provided for them to think together about their emotions, share the highs and lows of the teaching day, ask for support, acknowledge difficulties and share successes? Can they work through their anxieties with colleagues and come to accept themselves as well as each other? The quality of interaction between teachers and other staff needs as much care as that between teachers and students, and as much time allocated to it as there often is to the technical aspects of what they are required to deliver.

Case study 19 shows how it was the introduction of Quality Circle Time into the staff group at a demoralised primary school that led to a shift in the emotional atmosphere of the place. It enabled staff to take collective responsibility for what was happening. Case study 20 is an example of staff in a secondary school developing collective understanding through conversation.

Gerda Hanko describes in case study 21 how teachers can find new and creative ways of responding to young people when they share with each other the situations in which they find themselves. By meeting together regularly, teachers start to enhance their understanding of emotional factors in children's learning and to evolve new strategies for working with children whose behaviour causes concern.

The important point in all of this is to recognise that adults need the same opportunities as young people to practise emotional literacy. Only by engaging collaboratively with each other will they develop personally and professionally in ways that ensure they can play their full part in embedding emotional literacy within schools.

Case study 19

How Quality Circle Time changed the ways in which teachers at one primary school spoke to each other

Jack Lobley Primary School serves an area of high social deprivation in Tilbury, Essex. Children with special needs make up 50 per cent of the student population, which has a turnover rate of 10 per cent. The school was opened in 1972, and since then has had five head teachers. The current head has been in post for five years, and has appointed all but two of the 30 staff. (This article was written in 1998.)

Staffing ratios are high, with each class benefiting from a full-time teaching assistant. A central management team consists of the head and deputy, along with other post holders. All meetings are open to all staff. There are two staff meetings weekly, plus a management meeting on Wednesdays.

In 1993 Tilbury was named by HMI as an area failing to give children a quality education. The local press had labelled Tilbury as a 'Town of Dunces'. A barrage of criticism was directed at all the Tilbury schools by members of the local community.

Within the town, the four primary schools and one secondary joined together to develop an initiative designed to raise standards. This was backed up by additional funding and support.

In the third term of 1993, a new head teacher was appointed at Jack Lobley with a clear brief to improve behaviour at the school. At the time, too many children were exhibiting violent and aggressive behaviour both to staff and to each other. On several occasions, children had to be removed by the police.

Staff were demoralised and dysfunctional. It was difficult to recruit new people. Many teachers had been injured by children, and despite the best efforts of staff, there was no sense of support for each other, nor any sense of purpose in working with children. The head teacher decided to introduce Quality Circle Time into the school.

Implicit in the model is the need for schools to address behaviour management issues through supporting staff. By enabling individuals to share their visions of the school, to share the needs they have of a behaviour management system and to support each other in developing an ethos that allows a democratic voice for all, it engenders a sense of equal responsibility for all children among all staff.

At Jack Lobley, one of the first issues needing to be addressed was the lack of shared responsibility. Classes were organised purely according to numbers, and some classes consequently had several children with extreme behavioural problems while others had relatively few. Teachers took responsibility for their own children, and there was little mixing of staff between Key Stages 1 and 2.

In appointing a member of staff to the new post of Behaviour Coordinator, the head teacher went some way towards building on the strengths of individual staff. The person appointed was in her second year of teaching, and had gained some credibility as an NQT in being able to work with demanding children. As a team, the head and the behaviour coordinator agreed to hold monthly support meetings for staff to allow them to express their concerns about individual children and to focus on the needs of the school in developing a whole-school strategy.

At this stage, the school was still operating in crisis management mode, responding to the needs of children as situations arose. By implementing monthly meetings about behaviour management, staff were given the opportunity to express their concerns free of criticism and to feel listened to and valued.

It was also accepted at these meetings that responsibility for children rested not with the individual teacher, nor with the head teacher, but with all staff equally. It was by supporting each other through discussion, sharing and listening that a real impact could be made. Different strategies were discussed, and agreement was reached over using rules and rewards. Attention was turned to the possibility of using circle time as a strategy with children.

These meetings were a turning point. Through collective responsibility, an ethos was created in which children felt secure and where discipline was far more consistent. Teachers did not feel that they were on their own if their classes contained particularly difficult children. Also, responsibility did not rest solely with the head teacher, who previously had been expected to intervene at a stage when it was obvious that the child was out of control.

To this day, the single factor that is most noticeable about the school is the level of support that colleagues have for each other, and the opportunities for teachers to discuss the different strategies they employ with difficult children.

Alice Witherow (1998)

Case study 20

How a group of secondary teachers working with Antidote were helped to find a new way of talking to each other about teaching and learning

School staff often say that they have no time to talk about emotional literacy and what it might mean for their practice. But at one community school in the London Borough of Newham, 12 members of staff have been meeting with us for extended twilight sessions over the course of a term, and there are now plans to extend and expand the group.

It started with two 50-minute workshops on a training day for teaching staff. Some 35 people from departments across the school came to find out what we meant by emotional literacy, and what possible bearing it might have on classroom practice. By the end of the two sessions there was such energy in the room that we went back to the head teacher with a proposal. He agreed to pay colleagues who would commit to the equivalent of a day's work. When more volunteered than we had budgeted for, participants agreed to share out the money rather than lose their place in the process.

We started by asking what people felt about their work at the school. They all agreed that it aroused 'joy and despair', not always in equal measure. But there was heated debate about the causes of that despair.

Some pinpointed the constraints in the education system. One experienced teacher complained that the current curriculum 'stifles creativity and the freedom to learn and experiment'. Others argued that the curriculum is a useful guideline, that you can experiment within its parameters and find ways to make lessons 'memorable'. But where do teachers find the confidence to experiment, to be spontaneous, to take the risks you need to take to make a lesson 'emotionally rich'?

And is it unprofessional to try to make lessons 'fun'? A head of department argued that it is as important for her to enjoy the lessons as for her students, but she was uneasy about the language we were using: 'As a professional,' she said, 'I prefer to use "active learning" and "oracy" to communicate the issue of fun and participation.'

Others worried that real learning, real work, real life should not be 'fun'. Two comments were:

Kids should be made aware that the 'fun' inspired lessons they have at Key Stage 3 will not be carried through because it's basically all hard work for GCSE.

Life outside school and later on is tough and they need to be aware of this and prepared to work hard.

This led us into concerns about the home environment of many students:

Not many kids from this area go to university. The families are on income support or kids have free schools meals and they just don't make the connection that school gives them the opportunity to better themselves.

I am amazed by the limited horizons these kids have. They assume that life is the same everywhere else as it is in their community because they never go outside it.

And how some parents have passed on all responsibility for their children:

One parent I contacted asked me to keep his daughter in solitary confinement for two hours as he could not control or understand her either!

So how do teachers keep the high expectations that students deserve, while acknowledging the anxiety these expectations will raise in them and the behaviour that may trigger? In the second session we explored the emotional needs of learners, working from our own experience to identify key feelings and factors that make for a good or bad learning experience.

The group identified a core pattern in child development.

When you are younger, you can be very persistent (a teacher in this group remembered being five and trying for hours to use a skipping rope). As you get older you lose that confidence in yourself and become more self-conscious; so it feels less safe to make mistakes and try, try again.

Most of the group agreed that good relationships with teachers help learners to face challenging tasks. There was less agreement about what is the appropriate relationship. Do you meet the students on their own terms, or does that undermine your authority in the classroom? And is any relationship you have undermined by what they experience in other classrooms, particularly with supply teachers? Is it up to management to impose consistency, and how?

Relationships between students are also important, but what colleagues highlighted in this discussion were the interactions that seem to get in the way of learning. When one teacher complained, 'They think that school is a social club', another replied:

> At their age they don't think about lessons in relation to 'how much can I learn here?', they want to socialise with their friends and you have to tap into that somehow.

Another pointed to a group that is very motivated to achieve, but 'they don't seem comfortable with each other.' Is this something to do with the 'boffin culture'?

> There are some very clever kids in my tutor group but I think they are scared of coming out with comments for fear of bullying or being ridiculed by the others.

At the end of this session the group agreed to a small research task. The aim was to notice times when their students seemed more or less 'ready to learn', to observe what factors seemed to be in play, and to try one or two new approaches that might help students feel more connected and more confident in attempting challenging work.

When we reconvened four weeks later, it became clear that some of the group had forgotten the task. This led us into a discussion about how much energy teachers should put into trying to get children to do their homework. One teacher reported a successful strategy: she had created separate homework folders with a log sheet on the front and she regularly displays homework that shows good effort:

> From getting four or five to do the homework, I now get about 20 out of 30, so that's not bad!

A language teacher said that her students often say they did not do the homework because they did not understand it, 'which I don't accept. I am here every lunch-time and after school to help if they need it.' But a colleague pointed out that students can be 'too shy to be open about doing the work and how they feel about it; this is the area I pay attention to, the relationship with each individual.' He had experimented with reading out the names of people who arrived on time, handed in their work, thanked him when he helped them:

> All the little things. I don't tell them off for not doing them, but they notice when their name is not read out. The other day one boy put his hand up and said, 'Sir, I said thank you too, but I didn't say it loud enough.'

Another teacher had used a questionnaire to find out from her English as an additional language (EAL) students what kinds of work they preferred doing. In the next lesson she followed up with a class discussion and she is now rewriting the schemes of work to incorporate their suggestions. 'They can see that I am doing what they asked, and they are really working well.' With the same group, she started the year by negotiating the rules up front.

> We have a culture of respect, for example if they say something derogatory or racist then we discuss it and talk about the reasons why it was said, they don't just say it and get punished for it. I also tell them that it is okay to make mistakes in class, that I make mistakes too.

This threw up questions of authority and power for some.

> We all speak from our own perspectives and don't really take into account the other languages and cultures that some of us are used to. Some of the class see you as weak and soft if you are from another culture. It seems that they don't respect you if you don't shout enough.

Three members of the group met again with us to pull together the main points of debate and the practical ideas generated for use in the classroom. We are writing up a report to be shared with the group and then circulated to all colleagues. The head teacher has suggested that this group could meet with students from Year 9 who are researching their experience of school with our support. The small group was keen to do this and to involve parents as well.

Harriet Goodman (Antidote)

Case study 21

How one teacher found a solution to her classroom difficulties through collaborative problem-solving with fellow teachers

Nine-year-old Tony came from a single-parent family, a fact that had posed no apparent difficulties for him prior to the incident described here. He and his older brother were cared for by their father and paternal grandparents; their mother had been long out of the picture following a term of imprisonment which the boy and the school, but not his classmates, knew about. (Over 125,000 children in the UK have a parent in prison, but shame often forces them to hide the fact.) One day the subject of prison and related moral questions came up in class. Tony suddenly got up and told the class his mother had been in prison and now he did not know if she was alive or dead. He sat down, momentarily stunned by what he had done.

The next day Tony's behaviour altered radically from socially and intellectually competent to disruptive, unmanageable and bullying towards the other children, a deterioration that his teacher Mrs A found very distressing to watch. As a member of her school-based behaviour-focused support group, and in her concern to find an answer to addressing the situation, she put the question to her colleagues: What was Tony wanting her to do?

The teachers in this junior school already met regularly as a group initiated to enhance their understanding of emotional factors in children's learning and to discuss how to work with children whose behaviour was cause for concern. Following Mrs A's account of the story, the group explored the possible context of the incident: What might have led to it? What might it now mean to Tony to have told the whole world about the family secret? What might he now want from his teacher? Forty-five minutes of this kind of discussion deepened Mrs A's insight about Tony's likely needs gauged from his changed behaviour, as well as providing her with a sense of relief that others had been able to share her anxieties about Tony. A fortnight later she reported that two days after the discussion she had managed, after 'another awful day with Tony', to have a quiet talk with him. The conversation was carried on sympathetically and at behavioural level (i.e. not about Tony the person, but about Tony's behaviours). She offered her availability as a listening board for his feelings but assured him it was perfectly all right if he preferred to keep his feelings to himself. While Tony did not choose to take up Mrs A's offer, the consequence of this conversation was a reversal of his behaviour; Tony was again relating well to her and to the other children.

We could have left the matter at that, were the purpose of the group merely to give teachers an opportunity to get together to share their problems about dealing with specific cases. The matter was pursued, however. Intuitively Mrs A had understood his aggressive behaviour as a sign of panic and a message of distress. It was suggested to the group that the cessation of Tony's troublesome behaviour and his more relaxed way of relating to others might also be construed to show that he felt understood and that he had needed his feelings to be acknowledged. Furthermore this way of handling emotional upsets may also strengthen a child's coping capabilities for the future and help develop a repertoire of skills learned for solving them.

In subsequent group discussions the teachers also were asked to turn their thoughts to the father. We took into account how distressed he might be, if he had heard about the incident, at having the family secret spread all over the school through Tony's outburst. However, there was also evidence of the strength with which he cared for his sons. It was again left to Mrs A's discretion to see whether it was possible to involve the father without thereby adding to Tony's problems.

Having to solve problems like these can be a burden for teachers if insufficiently supported in their understanding of how children's family situations may adversely affect their progress at school but also to use such understanding in their relations with the children and in sensitive parent–teacher partnerships to enhance the children's progress. Mrs A, like her colleagues, had found their joint analysis of these issues thought-provoking, and considerations like these became a feature of their later case discussions.

Collaborative consultation meetings can be facilitated by a staff development tutor external to the school or by school-based curriculum or inclusion coordinators, a Special educational needs coordinator (SENCO) or pastoral care tutor. The specific joint problem-solving approach described here draws on the rich diversity of professional expertise which can be enhanced in every school, and the wide range of needs to be met in every classroom. Non-judgemental collegial sharing helps teachers to feel supported and cared about, invigorated by having their strengths acknowledged. Colleagues also enjoy the experience of offering creative support, adding to each other's and their own competence.

Gerda Hanko (1999)

I just want to ask ...

But when do we find the time to reflect on who we are, what we are doing together and what is going on between us?

This is partly about finding better ways to use existing time – recognising that unstructured discussions in staff meetings can lead to better use being made of the more structured elements. Partly it is about the way we use training days – for learning with and from each other, valuing and fostering what we know and can discover together – rather than relying on outsiders to introduce new sets of skills. And partly, too, it is about finding out that the sort of conversations we are talking about are important to us personally as well as professionally; so that it makes sense for us to make additional time for them to happen.

See Appendix 8 for organisations that promote emotional literacy training for teachers and others.

Students

Young people tend to respond with enthusiasm when they are offered safe opportunities to explore their emotions. They are keen to know what makes other people tick and they enjoy finding ways to work collaboratively with each other.

For particular individuals, different issues will cause them to feel safe or exposed. Some will only need to work through a natural reluctance to put their vulnerabilities on show; others will face formidable obstacles to sharing their experiences with others. Any emotional literacy strategy needs to take into account these different sensitivities.

Young people will respond more readily to opportunities for emotional literacy if they see modelled in the adults around them the same degree of openness and reflectiveness they are being asked to practise. It is indeed the extent to which teachers and other staff are able to show a capacity to process their own emotions that will determine how far young people themselves are willing to go.

Once conditions of safety have been established and young people understand what they are doing, then their main need is to be given some measure of control over the evolving process. They need to know that they can bring their imaginations, their capacity for empathy, their concern for each other to the task of generating a more emotionally literate environment.

It is the emotional climate of the organisation and the extent to which managers allow the various processes that encourage emotional literacy to grow and interact that will determine whether emotional literacy is a wave that steadily builds or one that quickly subsides.

Parents

The emotional literacy of young people is more likely to grow when their parents can help them negotiate the different messages they receive from school, their family and elsewhere. For this to happen, there needs to be a dynamic dialogue between the school and its parents.

Staff and parents have a common interest in ensuring that young people will find in their schools the stimulus they need to grow, achieve and experience well-being. This does not mean, though, that it is always easy for parents and staff to overcome the emotional blocks in the way of their partnership. Schools may find themselves struggling against the reluctance of those parents who had unsatisfactory experiences of school to become deeply involved in their own children's education. Parents may have reason to expect that a visit to the school will result in their being lectured. Some become locked, as a result, in a battle of mutual recrimination.

There are many schools that have found ways of overcoming these obstacles and ensuring that parents are keen to take part with teachers in thinking about how their children might grow emotionally and academically. Often this is about helping parents address their own emotional and learning needs as part of a process of becoming better able to address those of their children.

At **Tuckswood**, parents are invited to spend the first 20 minutes of every day working in the children's classes, and there are a variety of parent workshops and groups on offer. The aim is to ensure that there is a friendly and positive atmosphere in the school that leaves parents feeling relaxed enough to ask questions about what goes on in the school and how they can contribute.

Westborough too works hard at building links with students' homes. When children have not come to school, their parents are called. Teachers make home visits to parents who have not managed to attend meetings or whose children have not attended the school. Attendance at parent meetings is currently 98 per cent.

The engagement of a home-school support worker is one of the ways in which schools address the needs of parents in order to create opportunities for young people. The workers operate flexibly, seeking to find out why particular children may be having trouble getting to school or focusing on their learning then doing whatever they can to support the families in evolving appropriate strategies for addressing these issues.

Another model for engaging parents is the Family Links Nurturing Programme, described in case study 22. This a programme offered to parents, teachers and students as part of a process of exploring how emotional literacy might improve the quality of their lives. The value of this approach lies in the way all three groups involved develop their skills in parallel, creating the possibility that they will re-inforce each other's learning.

In this, as in everything else to do with emotional literacy, it is important to respond flexibly to the needs of the people one is trying to engage. A group of schools in Leicester recognised that parents, who come from many different cultures, were often discouraged from becoming actively engaged with the school because they lacked self-confidence. They responded by setting a series of family learning initiatives to draw in and engage their parents. Two days were put aside for mothers, and then fathers, to spend time in the school with their children telling stories about their own lives. These were followed by a series of events – a fair on health issues, two team-building days – designed to consolidate the relationships that had begun to evolve and help parents find ways to support their children's development.

These sorts of activities create opportunities for parents to find ways of talking about their feelings, to develop a sense that their problems can be shared and dealt with. Parents are helped to voice their frustrations and to overcome feelings of helplessness.

Case study 22

How the Family Links Nurturing Programme works to foster the skills associated with emotional literacy in parents, staff and children

The Family Links Nurturing Programme is a ten-week course designed for use in schools and with families. Developed in the US as a result of research undertaken by Dr Stephen Bavolek, a pioneer in the prevention of child abuse and neglect, and the development of family education, it offers an emotionally literate whole-school approach that promotes well-being in staff and pupils, a PSHE programme based on circle time, and a programme for parents.

The programme is based on four attitudes that promote emotional health: appropriate expectations of what a child can do at different ages and stages of development; self-awareness and self-esteem; positive approaches to discipline; and empathy. Emphasis is given to improving communication skills and to exploring emotions and the influence they have on behaviour, learning, relationships and health.

Schools introducing the Nurturing Programme undertake a two-day training for the entire staff (from head teachers to caretakers), which looks at the staff's emotional needs as well as those of the children in the school. The parent programme can be both a stand-alone programme as well as being used in conjunction with the children's programme.

Teachers report that the adoption of the programme techniques in their schools brings many benefits. There is a new sense of trust and teamwork among staff; schools in which staff morale tends to be low as they struggle with difficult or disruptive children are glad of practical help. Staff also have a chance to think about relationships with colleagues, and how kind or neglectful they are of themselves.

A key element of the programme is consistency. School staff value both the chance to enhance consistency in the way children's behaviour and the feelings that underlie it are handled within the school, and also the opportunity to build bridges with parents so as to extend this consistent approach into children's lives at home. Parents – some already quite confident, others who are struggling to raise their children – are glad both to have new ideas and to feel supported as they share experiences with other parents.

Research is supporting the feedback from schools and parents. An evaluation carried out by Mary Layton (1996) compared Wood Farm School, where the Nurturing Programme was being used, to a control school. She measured the extent to which the programme:

- empowered children to make responsible choices
- increased understanding and awareness of others
- taught positive ways of resolving conflict
- developed communication and social skills.

The evaluation found that there was significant improvement in the pro-social skills of the children on the programme over the six-month period assessed: the children at Wood Farm School improved considerably more throughout the six-month period than those at the control school. Further analysis of the results indicated that the programme improved the pro-social skills of the children not only in terms of school, but also in external situations. This suggested that the children had internalised the concepts of the programme and were able to apply their pro-social skills in a variety of situations.

Another study (Barlow and Stewart-Brown 2001) found that the programme had important benefits for parents. They valued the support they received, and gained confidence in themselves as parents (especially as a result of being able to think things through more calmly). They were also more able to empathise with their children and to understand why the children might behave in certain ways.

Candida Hunt (Family Links)

I just want to ask ...

But do schools really have the resources to involve parents in the way you are describing?

Schools that manage to involve parents actively find there are enormous benefits. So perhaps we are talking about the difficulty of setting up the sort of relationship that works and of imagining how any hurdles might be overcome. This will be different in every school, but it is likely to be about schools communicating to parents that they have something to offer them, that there is a genuine opportunity to participate and that it can benefit their children's behaviour as well as their learning. Often this is more about the school creating opportunities for the parents to provide things to each other than about doing anything specific themselves.

See Appendix 9 for groups providing support for parents and families.

LEAs

Local education authorities (LEAs) can help to ensure that schools have access to the information they need to inform their emotional literacy strategies and the resources they need to implement them. Using their knowledge of what is going on throughout the area, they can broker relationships between people who are trying to achieve similar objectives or who have complementary approaches.

Emotional literacy becomes sustainable in a school when staff, students, parents and the wider community engage in an ongoing conversation with each other about what is going on emotionally and how they want to respond to it. The most significant role for the LEA is to further strengthen this process by encouraging creative conversations between schools and the emergence of collaborative partnerships.

Schools need colleagues in other schools to perform the role of critical friends. It is easy for those who are inside an organisation to become so immersed in its daily struggles that they fail to spot things or they misread data. Having the chance to consider the situation with people who are in similar but different situations can help to reveal what is being missed.

Several authorities have followed the lead set by Southampton (case study 23) in setting up an Emotional Literacy Interest Group (ELIG) to create a network of head teachers and others with an interest in this area of work. The group provides a forum in which they can reflect together on the projects that will address the needs they have identified. The work of **Mason Moor Primary** described earlier in this book was one of the projects that emerged from the Southampton ELIG.

In Barrow-on-Furness (case study 24), the LEA provided crucial support to the educational psychology department in developing, piloting and promoting a behaviour curriculum designed to meet the needs identified by the area's primary schools. This was a project that effectively mobilised support at every level – parents, senior management, staff and students.

Case study 23

The Southampton experiment

Back in 1998, Southampton Education Authority took the forward-looking step of assigning emotional literacy the same level of importance as 'ordinary' literacy.

The strategy was championed by two people: Chief Inspector Ian Sandbrook and Principal Educational Psychologist Peter Sharp. They had read Daniel Goleman's book *Emotional Intelligence*, noted the then Education Minister Estelle Morris' statement that 'developing children as rounded people and active members of the community is at the heart of what schools are about' and concluded that the time might be right to reconsider the idea of education as a holistic enterprise.

Many who see emotional literacy as a way of motivating the learning or improving the behaviour of young people show some reluctance to practise what they are recommending to others. Sharp and Sandbrook, by contrast, began the Southampton programme by bringing together their fellow psychologists and inspectors for an exploration of their own life paths and vulnerabilities. Sharp has said:

> Starting with the self and taking time to 'stand and stare' is an important part of the process – understanding our own emotional literacy so that we may better promote the emotional literacy of our children.

This focus on staff promoting their own self-awareness has continued. Seminars, presentations and development events are held regularly for managers, who are 'expected to incorporate this work into section plans with measurable outcomes'. The outcomes anticipated include not only improvements in efficiency and effectiveness, but also more positive attitudes to work, increased realism about what is possible and an improved work-life balance – working smarter rather than harder.

Once people within the LEA had accepted the need for emotional literacy to flow from the top, Southampton's heads were offered an opportunity to find out more. Gratifyingly, some 90 per cent of head teachers came along to the seminars and responded positively to what they had heard. Some of them then signed up for the Southampton Emotional Literacy Interest Group (SELIG), which was set up to take the intiative forward. Also included in SELIG are some deputy heads, senior teachers, educational psychologists, inspectors, a PSHE teacher adviser, a consultant psychiatrist, some governors and a representative from Southampton University.

The group has published its Guidelines for Promoting Emotional Literacy, based on the initial results from projects in 12 schools. A web-based NELIG (National Emotional Literacy Interest Group – www.nelig.co.) has been set up. Looking a few years ahead, there are plans to produce curriculum materials, to set up a resource bank and to publish models for good practice in schools, education services and multi-agency settings.

Stages in the development of Southampton's emotional literacy strategy

- Establish a partner to champion the strategy
- Begin with the individual
- Provide an awareness-raising programme of seminars, presentations and publications
- Promote the idea that emotional literacy is a priority
- Set up an Emotional Literacy Interest Group
- Undertake demonstration or pilot projects in schools
- Plan evaluation or implementation of emotional literacy strategy
- Incorporate emotional literacy into all major plans – Emotional Development Plan, behaviour support, children's services, early years etc.

Southampton Emotional Literacy Guidelines (2002)

Case study 24

How Barrow-in-Furness developed a curriculum focused on emotional and social skills

The Furness project worked from the assumption that all students need to be taught the skills, values and abilities that underpin positive behaviour and emotional competence.

A team of people led by senior educational psychologist Deborah Michel developed a curriculum that focused on emotional and social skills. The idea was to come up with something that could be integrated with the National Curriculum as it was being implemented in each school.

In calling this approach The Behaviour Curriculum, they wanted to encourage schools to see behaviour not as something responded to when it was dysfunctional, but rather as something that schools took responsibility for developing.

Once the basic curriculum document had been prepared, a series of workshops was then offered to primary teachers who took responsibility for cascading these ideas through their own school staff.

All eight primary schools that took part in the project during 1998–2000 were situated in a coastal region where high unemployment has resulted in considerable social deprivation and poverty. They utilised a wide range of learning activities for teaching aspects of the curriculum. These included assemblies, structured lessons and unstructured sessions such as play and dinner times. In each school, there were differences in the length of sessions and the time of day they were offered. Factors such as Ofsted inspections, staffing or other pressures tended to limit the time available.

LEA support was essential. There was money invested in training time and supply cover for teachers in the project schools, together with the provision of extra resources for materials. The Behaviour Curriculum pack was marketed to schools within the LEA that were not part of the original pilot phase. An occasional newsletter was produced by the LEA that reported on the initiative and disseminated information.

 The major vehicle that all the schools used for the transmission of the Curriculum was circle time. This afforded the children the opportunity to bring to the group anything that they wanted to raise, including both personal concerns and school events.

In most cases, these were handled sensitively. Children were given space and time to talk. The prevailing atmosphere was one of peace, calm and quiet. Some of the children who interrupted were admonished by their peers. Others adjusted their own behaviour. Great emphasis was put by the children on adhering to the rules that they had formulated for their own classroom and for school. Most of the children saw these sessions as enjoyable and fun and were also conscious that they formed an important part of their school day.

All the schools promoted a number of ways of ensuring parental participation. A couple of schools encouraged parents to participate in circle time or to work with individuals on related topics. In one school, parents had decorated the room that was to be used for circle time. One head teacher reported involving parents through an art project where they had worked with the children through music, dancing and making things. This culminated in building a float for a procession.

Teachers saw the support of head teachers for the innovation, and effective leadership in its introduction, as crucial. They needed to articulate an agreement with the underlying premiss of the innovation: that successful learning for all pupils could be enhanced by the adults modelling positive behaviour in and out of lessons and by developing positive teaching strategies for the children. They needed to believe that this would increase the motivation of children to learn and to engage in cooperative behaviour.

As the innovation is meant to be holistic, its success depends upon the commitment of staff, their positive attitudes and an inclusive ethos. Where a whole staff engaged in training, relationships altered subtly. Putting on a programme of staff training had allowed opportunities for the adults to reflect on current practice, identify common issues and engage in positive discussions about how to manage processes.

Positive commitment to the curriculum had important implications for the relationships between teachers and pupils. They were able to gain additional insight into the relationships between the children and any conflicts they were engaged in. It offered opportunities for the children to challenge each other about certain issues in a safe, blame-free and managed environment. Some teachers said it had enabled them to see some of their children in a very different light. Having the chance to sit in a relaxed way with the children also altered the classroom dynamics in various ways.

Listening to the children was often revelatory and most of the teachers looked forward with pleasure to these sessions. Some teachers mentioned they had thought much more deeply about using different kinds of teaching methods for different processes and exploring ways of working to accommodate different learning styles. One teacher commented that it was noticeable how assertive some of the normally shy or withdrawn children had become and how some of the normally aggressive children had become much more calm.

Generally, the interviewees were convinced that the inception of the Behaviour Curriculum had positively affected the quality of relationships between the children. Levels of aggression were lower, conflicts and confrontations were lessened, and consequent motivation, willingness to work and work output of the children was enhanced. The children seemed more willing to listen to each other, and could be seen to be employing some of the skills and strategies that were being 'taught' during the focused sessions.

One teacher felt that the framework of the Behaviour Curriculum enabled him to focus more clearly on 'how to teach' and to think about the thoughts and feelings of the class group and consequent social relationships. He said he thought that if children felt safe, then they would be more likely to take risks in their learning.

Some schools said that the 'performance' of the children and improvements in cognitive development were a direct result of implementing the curriculum. Although difficult to measure by statistical means, there was a tangible impact that could be observed during the learning process. Children seemed much more inclined to take responsibility for their own learning and 'to share things, to listen to each other and to work towards a common goal'.

According to some of the teachers, language acquisition and use had been significantly enhanced. Children were much more patient in allowing the less articulate members of the class time to express themselves. Allowing children opportunities to explore their feelings about certain subjects and issues had improved the quality of their expressive language and grammatical accuracy. This had a spin-off for their writing as well. Children were using longer and more complex sentences in the work they produced. The children were also prepared to be more inclusive, to allow fellow pupils previously shunned at playtimes to join in with them. Some even made positive moves to encourage them to join in.

One of the central strands of the curriculum is to engender in the children high self-esteem, motivation and positive behaviour through modelling and by teaching them the requisite skills. The adults who work with the children are seen as the main conduit through which the process is taught and assimilated.

For those adults who were actively interested and involved, the quality of teaching and social interaction were significantly enhanced. Some said it had raised their awareness of not only the antecedents of certain behaviours, but it had made them focus upon feelings and emotions, the impact upon the children and their relationships.

Qualities identified by the adults from training were:

- heightened level of sensitivity to the children and other adults
- added stimulation from considering old problems from new angles
- new ideas and support for innovative practice
- greater opportunities for openness and examination of personal attitudes to real issues
- the necessity for periods of reflection to assess new ideas
- greater flexibility of working practices.

Helen Channon (2000)

Government

Governments face considerable difficulties in trying to play a positive role in the promotion of emotional literacy in schools.

Foremost among these is the challenge of managing society's anxieties about whether our schools are any good, whether children are learning and whether they are going to develop a sense of personal morality. In seeking to show that they are addressing these anxieties, it is easy for ministers to become drawn into declaring that they will be tough on incompetent teachers, take firm action to remove disorder from our streets and promote strategies that can raise levels of academic achievement. All too often, the result is that teachers end up with the sense that they are being told what they should teach and what students should learn in a way that undermines any explicit commitments to encouraging the professionalism of teachers or the creativity and sense of responsibility of their students.

Different policy initiatives seek to tackle the various problems that face schools. There are initiatives for mental health and emotional well-being, for disaffection and thinking skills, for teachers' morale and for school leadership. Sitting amid these fragments, it can be difficult to see that the challenges they are tackling are the same – the feeling among teachers and their students that they are not fully trusted or respected.

Emotional literacy is a strategy for creating environments in schools where policy-makers do not feel the need to tell people what to do because there are evidently effective processes for negotiating what needs to be learned, how it is going to be learned, and how people are going to collaborate in improving the quality of their teaching and learning.

If government is to foster the development of such approaches, it needs to go with the same emotionally literate grain. That means trying to avoid telling people what to do and how to do it, finding ways instead to foster environments that motivate people to learn and enable them to find the most effective ways of doing so.

To achieve that, ministers and officials need to collect up stories of change, listen to them, learn from them, channel them to the places where they can raise people's vision of what is possible and engage in active reflection about what new ways to do things they suggest. Their most important role is to help people identify their strengths, understand their problems, tackle their difficulties and discover creative ways of moving forward.

5

Conclusion – education for an emotionally literate society

Our school system was designed for a society that was relationship rich and information poor. To thrive in the very different circumstances of today, we need to develop schools that will nurture people's capacity to connect with each other. Only by doing this can we ensure they are able to process the wealth of information that is available to them – to learn from it, make sense of it and find in it the keys to a strong sense of personal purpose.

Emotional literacy is a vital part of this process because it helps people to develop their capacities for managing the uncertainties that are inherent in modern living, and to become energised by the opportunities to participate in changing things for the better. It does so by broadening the range of what they are able to think about and talk about.

By embedding emotional literacy in the everyday practice of our schools, we will enhance young people's capacity to realise their potential and experience wellbeing, while at the same time fostering the qualities that help them build strong relationships, have fulfilling experiences of work and play an engaged part in the lives of their communities.

By letting the practice of emotional literacy grow out from our schools – carried by young people, their parents, teachers and other staff – we create the possibility that emotional literacy can start to become more deeply embedded in the wider culture, so that people will start to look for opportunities to engage with others in ways that build emotional understanding and facilitate the transformation of angry and anxious states into productive activity.

As emotional literacy spreads, it has the potential to help people listen more attentively to themselves and to each other, to understand their own needs more deeply, to explore with others how these needs can be met through changes in the world around them and what contribution they can make to those changes.

Emotional literacy can help to build communities that encourage neighbours to connect with each other; workplaces that cultivate creativity and draw upon our potential to contribute; and a political process that engages us in its deliberations and is responsive to the ideas that emerge. In all these ways, emotional literacy engages people in seeking creative responses to the challenges of their time.

In rising to the challenge of embedding emotional literacy in our schools, therefore, students, teachers and other staff are taking on the extremely important task of trying to build a more harmonious, energised and sustainably prosperous society.

Antidote's work

The ideas contained in this book reflect the thinking that has developed over the past three years as a small group of people, brilliantly coordinated by Antidote's Education Director Harriet Goodman, have taken forward a project designed to work out how emotional literacy can become more firmly established in primary and secondary schools.

The project grew out of Antidote's Fourth R conference in the spring of 1998, a year after the conference mentioned in the introduction. At the second event, participants explored a range of processes designed to enhance the emotional and social skills of young people. In the process, they identified the need to develop further our understanding of how schools might determine:

1 which practices were appropriate to their needs;
2 how these practices might be adapted to address those needs more effectively;
3 how different practices might be integrated to achieve a cumulative benefit;
4 how the implementation of these practices could have, over time, a sustainable impact on teaching, learning, behaviour and well-being.

The first stage of this work, which began in the autumn of 2001, involved us conducting an in-depth survey of our project schools to identify what factors influenced the capacity of staff and students to communicate with each other in ways that would enhance emotional literacy and promote achievement. The analysis of this data was used to develop an Emotional Literacy Audit (ELA) tool as a more streamlined process for building a picture of a school's emotional climate. This addressed particularly the elements described in the section on the **qualities of an emotionally literate school.**

The results of the audit are fed back, as the survey results were in the project schools, to focus groups across the schools. The aim is to stimulate discussion about how to evolve a whole-school emotional literacy strategy that will enhance the practices already in place and lead to the development of new ones.

At the project schools, this led on to interventions at all levels. We worked with senior management and staff on issues around communication, teamworking and teaching styles. We helped staff and students develop strategies for using enquiry and dialogue to stimulate young people's interest in each other and in what they were learning. We set up groups of young people to address ways of fostering a culture in which they would take more responsibility for their relationships with each other, for their learning and for the overall work of the school.

Halfway through this three-year project, this work was clearly beginning to have a positive impact on factors such as staff capacity to take up their creativity and students' engagement in learning. This encouraged us to develop a programme of training and consultancy to share with schools across the UK what we are learning about how to foster more emotionally literate school environments.

For information on Antidote's services and activities, call 020 7247 3355, send an email to emotional.literacy@antidote.org.uk or take a look at www.antidote.org.uk.

Organisations offering processes for developing emotional language

Children and Youth Partnership Foundation
54–56 Euston Street
London NW1 2ES
T: 020 7504 1111
F: 020 7388 4758
E: info@cypf.org
W: www.CYPF.org
W: www.makeaconnection.org.uk

CYPF designs and implements innovative programmes that support the positive development of children and young people. One of these programmes, Making a Connection, is described in Chapter 2.

Equal Voice (Pop-Up Theatre)
27a Brewery Road
London N7 9PU
T: 020 7609 3339
F: 020 7609 2284
E: admin@equalvoice.net
W: www.equalvoice.net
W: www.pop-up.net

Pop-Up Theatre's Equal Voice programme is a collection of drama techniques that teachers can use to address situations of conflict. The mainstream work consists of training teachers by direct work with their class and follow-up support.

Lapidus
BM Lapidus
London WC1N 3XX
E: info@lapidus.org.uk
W: www.lapidus.org.uk

Lapidus is a membership organisation which promotes the use of the literary arts for personal development. It works with health authorities, libraries, and schools.

Learning Through Action
 Fair Cross
 Stratfield Saye
 Nr Reading RG7 2BT
 T: 01256 883500
 F: 01256 883700
 E: info@learning-through-action.org.uk
 W: www.learning-through-action.org.uk

LTA uses structured role play and associated techniques to work with schools on challenging preconceptions, stimulating thinking and promoting a new approach to personal decision-making. In this way, it aims to help overcome the causes of alienation and under-performance.

National Institute of Adult Continuing Education
 21 DeMontfort Street
 Leicester LE1 7GE
 T: 0116 204 4200/4201
 F: 0116 285 4514
 E: enquiries@niace.org.uk
 W: www.niace.org.uk

NIACE is a non-governmental organisation that promotes adult learning. Its Young Adult Learners Partnership (YALP) with the National Youth Agency developed the Getting Connected curriculum described in Chapter 2.

Partnership for Children
 26–27 Market Place
 Kingston upon Thames
 Surrey KT1 1JH
 T: 020 8974 6004
 F: 020 8974 6600
 E: info@partnershipforchildren.org.uk
 W: www.partnershipforchildren.org.uk

Partnership for Children works to improve the emotional well-being of children and young people around the world. It took over from Befrienders International the programme called *Zippy's Friends* (see case study 2).

TACADE
 Old Exchange Building
 St Ann's Passage
 Manchester M2 6AF
 T: 0161 836 6850
 F: 0161 836 6859
 E: info@tacade.co.uk
 W: www.tacade.com

TACADE undertakes research and produces a wide range of resources for use by professionals, parents, communities and young people. These range from materials on drugs, smoking, alcohol and substance abuse to life skills programmes.

Theatr Fforwm Cymru
 Goodwick Community Centre
 New Hill
 Goodwick
 Pembs SA64 ODR
 T: 01348 873805
 F: 01348 873805
 E: fforwm@aol.com

Using a mixture of forum theatre, circle time, open-space technology, active listening skills and other related techniques, the company helps school and community groups understand themselves, others and the wider world.

Up Front Theatre
 2a Bishopdale Road
 Lancaster
 Lancashire LA1 5NF
 T: 01524 849756
 E: ceri&chris@upfronttheatre.freeserve.co.uk

Provides, participatory workshops and projects, and training using theatre, performance and media arts. They work with groups who may not normally have the opportunity to appreciate, learn and speak through the arts.

Organisations promoting or offering training in circle time

Lucky Duck Publishing Ltd
3 Thorndale Mews
Clifton
Bristol BS8 2HX
T: 0117 9732881
F: 0117 9731707
E: publishing@luckyduck.co.uk
W: www.luckyduck.co.uk

Publishers of books, videos and other resources. They also provide training on circle time emphasising that it is not a behaviour management intervention but a way of teaching morality, tolerance, values and ethics.

Jenny Mosley Consultancies/Positive Press Ltd
28a Gloucester Road
Trowbridge
Wiltshire BA14 0AJ
T: 01225 719204
F: 01225 755631
E: circletime@jennymosley.demon.co.uk
W: www.circle-time.co.uk

The Whole School Quality Circle Time Model introduces the school community to a range of approaches designed to encourage emotional and physical safety, consistency, motivation, positive relationships and openness. It has, at its heart, a commitment to building children's self-worth and helping them to care more about the feelings of others.

Organisations that promote or provide training in peer support

Childline in Partnership with Schools
ChildLine
45 Folgate Street
London E1 6GL
T: 020 7650 3200
F: 020 7650 3201
E: hqchips@childline.org.uk
W: www.childline.org.uk

CHIPS provides schools, voluntary and statutory organisations with information about issues that affect young people, resources such as leaflets and fact sheets as well as workshops on bullying and how to set up peer support schemes. They also train students to be peer supporters.

Conflict and Change
2a Streatfield Avenue
East Ham
London E6 2LA
T: 020 8552 2050
F: 020 8470 5505
E: conflict_change@btconnect.com
W: www.conflictandchange.co.uk

The organisation helps schools to develop a clear, consistent approach to the difficulties experienced by staff and students as part of a behaviour policy which includes anti-bullying strategies and a supportive pastoral system.

***Leap* Confronting Conflict**
8 Lennox Road
Finsbury Park
London N4 3NW
T: 020 7272 5630
F: 020 7272 8405
E: info@leaplinx.com
W: www.leaplinx.com

Provides opportunities for young people to explore creative approaches to conflicts in their lives. Projects include: Quarrel Shop; Young Mediators' Network; Gangs and Territorialism; Leadership with Young Offenders; and Conflict in Schools. *Leap* also run training courses for adults and produce a number of publications and resources.

Mediation UK
Alexander House
Telephone Avenue
Bristol BS1 4BS
T: 0117 904 6661
F: 0117 904 3331
E: enquiry@mediationuk.org.uk
W: www.mediationuk.org.uk

A national voluntary organisation dedicated to developing constructive means of resolving conflicts in communities. Trainers around the country work with primary and secondary schools to train adults and pupils in how to sort out disputes in in the quickest, most creative way.

Mental Health Foundation
83 Victoria Street
London SW1H OHW
T: 020 7802 0300
F: 020 7802 0301
E: mhf@mhf.org.uk
W: www.mentalhealth.org.uk

MHF supports seven schools and colleges in London to develop peer support projects with the aim of promoting the mental health of children and young people.

National Coalition Building Institute (UK)
The Learning Exchange
Wygston's House
Applegate
Leicester LE1 5LD
T: 0116 222 9977
F: 0116 222 9970
E: info@ncbileic.org.uk
W: www.ncbiuk.org.uk

The NCBI is dedicated to ending the mistreatment of all groups, whether it be because of nationality, race, class, gender, religion, sexual orientation, age, physical ability, occupation or life circumstances.

The Peer Support Forum
National Children's Bureau
8 Wakley Street
London EC1V 7QE
T: 020 7843 6000
F: 020 7278 9512
E: peersupportforum@ncb.org.uk
W: www.ncb.org.uk/psf

The aim of the PSF is to promote peer support as a process of enhancing and developing the social and emotional well-being of children and young people in schools and other settings.

Peer Support Works
11 Brunswick Terrace
Stafford ST16 1BB
T: 01785 613585/07967 332741
F: 0870 13326238
E: info@peersupportworks.com
W: www.peersupportworks.com

Provides peer support and other customised services for schools, educational institutions and workplaces where people of all ages are trained in anti-bullying, peer support, mediation, assertiveness and other PSHE issues.

Trust for the Study of Adolescence
23 New Road
Brighton BN1 1WZ
T: 01273 693311
F: 01273 679907
E: info@tsa.uk.com
W: www.tsa.uk.com

TSA seeks to improve the lives of young people through research, conferences, training and publications. It has run projects on youth empowerment, youth offending and mental health.

Young Voice
12 Bridge Gardens
East Molesey
Surrey KT8 9HU
F: 020 89792952
E: info@young-voice.org
W: www.young-voice.org

A voluntary organisation which aims to make the views of young people heard. Consultation, research and training are offered along with easy-to-read publications and research reports. Offering young people's views on bullying, depression, divorce, etc.

Organisations that provide training in philosophy for children

Centre for Thinking Skills
Brunel University
300 St Margarets Road
Twickenham TW1 1PT
T: 020 8891 0121
F: 020 8891 8270
E: robert.fisher@brunel.ac.uk
W: www.teachingthinking.net

Offers talks, workshops, seminars, presentations and resources for teachers and others concerned with improving the thinking, learning and creativity of children.

Dialogue WORKS
The Old School Business Centre
Newport
Pembrokeshire SA42 0TS
T: 01239 820440
E: enquiries@dialogueworks.co.uk
W: www.dialogueworks.co.uk

Dialogue Works brings together leading trainers in critical thinking and creative dialogue to run conferences and training for teachers or students. Their consultants include leading Philosophy for Children practitioners across all key stages.

SAPERE (Society for the Advancement of Philosophical Enquiry and Reflection in Education)
3 Abbotts Close
Winchester SO23 7EY
T: 01962 853 516
E: rogersutcliffe@onet.co.uk
W: www.sapere.net

SAPERE trains and supports teachers in developing 'communities of philosophical enquiry', seeing this as a way to enrich the lives of young people – enabling them to explore their diverse perspectives, values and philosophies in a caring and collaborative manner.

Organisations that provide therapeutic group work or relevant training

Atlow Mill Centre for Emotional Education
Hognaston
Nr Ashbourne
Derbyshire DE6 1PX
T: 01335 370494
F: 01335 370279
E: centre@atlowmill.ndo.co.uk
W: www.atlowmill.ndo.co.uk

Atlow Mill works with young people who have been identified as being at risk of permanent exclusion from school. Residential programmes encourage young people to identify the side of themselves that causes problems for them. The Mill also runs a postgraduate certificate in emotional education.

Caspari Foundation
Caspari House
1 Noel Road
The Angel
Islington
London N1 8HQ
T: 020 7704 1977
F: 020 7704 1783
E: admin@caspari.org.uk
W: www.caspari.org.uk

Provides educational therapy for children with emotional, behavioural and learning difficulties, and consultations to their families/carers/teachers. The Foundation aims to promote insight into emotional factors in learning and provides part-time courses (MA, Aspects), INSET lectures and conferences.

The Child Psychotherapy Trust
Star House
104–108 Grafton Road
London NW5 4BD
T: 020 7284 1355
F: 020 7284 2755
E: cpt@globalnet.co.uk
W: www.childpsychotherapytrust.org.uk

The Trust works to increase awareness of the ideas and values of child psychotherapy; to promote understanding of children's emotional health and to increase access to local child and adolescent psychotherapy services for young people in need. It publishes leaflets and other materials.

Coram Family
49 Mecklenburgh Square
London WC1N 2QA
T: 020 7520 0300
E: reception@coram.org.uk
W: www.coram.org.uk

Coram Family works with vulnerable children and young people to promote resilience, enabling them to take responsibility for their own lives and achieve their full potential.

Counselling in Education
1 Regent Place
Rugby
Warwickshire CV21 2PJ
T: 0870 4435170
F: 0870 4435160
E: gemma.green@bacp.co.uk
W: www.cie.uk.com

Counselling in Education is a specialist division of the BACP (British Association for Counselling and Psychotherapy). It exists to promote and support the counselling of young people in educational and youth organisations.

National Pyramid Trust
84 Uxbridge Road
London W13 8RA
T: 020 8579 5108
F: 020 8579 5108
E: enquiries@nptrust.org.uk
W: www.nptrust.org.uk

The NPT helps primary school-aged children to fulfil their potential in school and in life by building their self-esteem and resilience. The Trust, through local partnerships of statutory and voluntary agencies, runs programmes for seven- to ten-year-olds who are causing concern.

The Place2Be
Wapping Telephone Exchange
Royal Mint Street
London E1 8LQ
T: 020 7780 6189
E: enquiries@theplace2be.org.uk
W: www.theplace2be.org.uk

P2B provides early intervention through emotional and therapeutic support to children within the school environment. The difficulties that children present who access The Place2Be include: hyperactivity, disruptive and aggressive behaviours, peer difficulties, sadness and anxiety.

Total Learning Challenge
  Ouseburn Building
  Albion Row
  East Quayside
  Newcastle on Tyne NE6 ILL
  T: 0191 275 5023
  F: 0191 275 5024
  E: enquiry@total-learning.org.uk
  W: www.total-learning.org.uk

TLC provides action group skills interventions for children identified as being at risk of disaffection. The organisation works in partnership with schools facilitating change in staff approaches to handling children. In addition they offer modular training in therapeutic group work at the University of Northumbria, and bespoke training.

YoungMinds
  102–108 Clerkenwell Road
  London EC1M 5SA
  T: 020 7336 8445
  Parents Info Service: 0800 018 2138
  F: 020 7336 8446
  E: enquiries@youngminds.org.uk
  W: www.youngminds.org.uk

YoungMinds is the national charity committed to improving the mental health of all babies, children and young people. Its Parents' Information Service is for any adult with concerns about the mental health of a child or young person. Other services include training, consultancy and publications.

Organisations with an interest in emotionally literate ways of learning

Campaign for Learning
19 Buckingham Street
London WC2N 6EF
T: 020 7930 1111
F: 020 7930 1551
E: gphyall@cflearning.org.uk
W: www.campaign-for-learning.org.uk

The Campaign works to create an appetite for learning in every individual and to foster a learning society. Their vision is of an inclusive society in which learning is valued, understood, enjoyed, wanted and widely available to everyone.

The Circle Works
6 Temple Yard
Temple Street
Bethnal Green
London E2 6QD
T: 020 7729 9671
E: geoffreycourt@classicfm.net
E: jeannetteweaver@beeb.net

Working with children, The Circle Works is an educational charity based in east London, and seeks to understand the conditions that enable effective dialogue.

Education Extra
17 Old Ford Road
London E2 9PL
T: 020 8709 9900
F: 020 809 9933
E: info@educationextra.org.uk
W: www.educationextra.org.uk

Education Extra provides advice, resources, information and support about out-of-school-hours learning. Its purpose is to enable schools to work with pupils, their families and the wider community.

Education Now
113 Arundel Drive
Bramcote Hills
Nottingham NG9 3FQ
T: 0115 925 7261
F: 0115 925 7261
E: edheretics@gn.apc.org
W: www.educationnow.gn.apc.org

Education Now is a cooperative devoted to developing a more flexible education system to cope with the wide variety of learning styles and forms of intelligence as well as the needs of a rapidly changing society.

Human Scale Education
Unit 8
Fairseat Farm
Chew Stoke, Bristol
BS40 8XF
T: 01275 332516
F: 01275 332516
E: info@hse.org.uk
W: www.hse.org.uk

HSE believes that the child should be at the centre of the educational process, and that schools and classes need to be small in size in order to provide a supportive learning environment. HSE campaigns for state funding to go to new educational initiatives, and supports large schools in finding ways to restructure into small learning communities.

Re:membering Education
66 Beaconsfield Villas
Brighton BN1 6HE
T: 01273 239311
F: 01273 239311
E: remember@mcmail.com
W: www.remember.mcmail.com

Re:membering Education believes that at the heart of education is how we help young people make connections between their own experience and the curriculum. They offer strategic advice on the shaping, implementation and review of policy.

SEAL – Society for Effective Affective Learning
37 Park Hall Road
East Finchley
London N2 9PT
T: 020 8365 3869
F: 020 8444 0339
E: seal@seal.org.uk
W: www.seal.org.uk

SEAL's mission is to promote learning approaches that embrace body, emotions, mind and spirit to enable people to develop their full potential. Activities include international conferences, information and materials, journals and newsletters, workshops and seminars.

Steiner Waldorf Schools Fellowship
Kidbroooke Park
Forest Row
East Sussex RH18 5JB
T: 01342 822115
F: 01342 826004
E: mail@swsf.org.uk
W: www.steinerwaldorf.org.uk

Steiner schools are committed to the principle that a child's 'emotional and social skills' should be at the centre of all educational practice. The aim is to equip pupils to respond with initiative, flexibility and responsibility in a fast-changing world.

University of the First Age
Millennium Point
Curzon Street
Digbeth, Birmingham B4 7XG
T: 0121 202 2347
F: 0121 202 2384
E: marilyn_o'neill@birmingham.gov.uk
W: www.ufa.org.uk

The University offers young people transferring to secondary school an opportunity to take part in vacation- and distance-learning experiences that expose them to a curriculum that extends and enriches whatever is already happening in the school environment.

Organisations promoting democracy, citizenship and values education in schools

Association for Citizenship Teaching
C/o The Citizenship Foundation
Ferroners House
Shaftesbury Place, Aldersgate Street
London EC2Y 8AA
T: 020 7367 0510
F: 020 7367 0501
E: info@teachingcitizenship.org.uk
W: www.teachingcitizenship.org.uk

ACT is the professional association for those engaged in promoting citizenship education in England. The association aims to support the work of practitioners, strengthen support networks and partnerships, and encourage research in relevant areas.

Centre for Citizenship Studies in Education
School of Education
21 University Road
Leicester LE1 7RF
T: 0116 252 3681
F: 0116 252 3653
E: ccse@le.ac.uk
W: www.le.ac.uk/education/centres/citizenship

The Centre provides information on all aspects of citizenship education and training. It is committed to developing more democratic and inclusive approaches to education, based on the principles of freedom, equality, justice and peace. It aims to support schools as model communities, in which there is respect for the individual and for difference, and for equality of rights.

Changemakers
Baybrook Farm
Lower Godney
Nr Wells
Somerset BA5 1RZ
T: 01458 834767
F: 01458 830588
E: info@changemakers.org.uk
W: www.changemakers.org.uk

Changemakers enables young people to lead positive change through tackling issues of concern to themselves, their community and the world in which they live. It is a nationwide organisation enabling young people actively to design projects which they themselves manage, help resource and review.

The Citizenship Foundation
Ferroners House
Shaftesbury Place
Aldersgate Street
London EC2Y 8AA
T: 020 7367 0500
F: 020 7367 0501
E: info@citfou.org.uk
W: www.citizenshipfoundation.org.uk

The Citizenship Foundation encourages informed and active citizenship, especially among young people. Current teaching materials extend from primary to upper secondary levels. The Foundation is building on its expertise to develop a wide range of resources and provide training programmes, and a network of support for teachers.

CSV Education
237 Pentonville Road
London N1 9NJ
T: 020 7278 6601
F: 020 7713 0560
E: education@csv.org.uk
W. www.csv.org.uk

Creates opportunities for young people in schools, colleges and universities to play an active part in their community. It provides books, training and a dedicated web site to support teachers, lecturers and students in developing active citizenship and community involvement.

Institute for Citizenship
62 Marylebone High Street
London W1U 5HZ
T: 020 7935 4777
F: 020 7486 9212
E: info@citizen.org.uk
W: www.citizen.org.uk

The Institute aims to promote informed, active citizenship and greater participation in democracy and society by developing innovative programmes for citizenship education, encouraging voter participation and stimulating debate.

Institute for Global Ethics
3–4 Bentinck Street
London W1U 2EE
T: 020 7486 1954
F: 020 7935 3486
E: igeuk@globalethics.org.uk
W: www.globalethics.org.uk

The Institute is dedicated to promoting ethical fitness through public discourse and practical action. The UK Trust is the British entity of the Institute of Global Ethics, founded in the US in 1990.

The National Youth Agency
17–23 Albion Street
Leicester LE1 6GD
T: 0116 285 3700
F: 0116 285 3777
E: nya@nya.org.uk
W: www.nya.org.uk

The NYA's main aim is to support youth work and informal education. The agency promotes young people's personal and social development, as well as their voice, influence and place in society.

The Princes Trust
18 Park Square East
London NW1 4LH
T: 0800 842842
F: 020 7543 1200
E: info@princes-trust.org.uk
W: www.princes-trust.org.uk

The Trust runs a series of projects that help to foster the self-confidence, motivation and resilience of young people aged 14 to 30 who are in challenging circumstances and face significant barriers to success.

School Councils UK
2nd Floor
Lawford House
5 Albert Place
London N3 1QB
T: 020 8349 2459
F: 020 8346 0898
E: info@schoolcouncils.org
W: www.schoolcouncils.org

School Councils UK provide training and resources to help teachers and students set up school councils and develop into caring communities.

Values Education Council
College House
51–54 Hockley Hill
Birmingham B18 5AQ
T: 021 515 4526
E: values@vecuk.org.uk
W: www.vecuk.org.uk

Promotes and develops values education, as part of a strategy for helping individuals develop as responsible and caring members of a pluralist society.

Organisations that provide emotional literacy training for teachers and others

Antidote
3rd Floor, Cityside House
40 Adler Street
Aldgate East
London E1 1EE
T: 020 7247 3355
F: 020 7247 7992
E: emotional.literacy@antidote.org.uk
W: www.antidote.org.uk

Antidote offers training and consultancy to secondary and primary schools, as well as LEAs and other educational organisations around the country, on ways of using emotional literacy to enhance learning, behaviour and well-being. Services offered include:
- workshops for school staff
- workshops for school leaders
- workshop series for teaching staff
- consultancy to staff teams
- development of a whole-school emotional literacy strategy using the Emotional Literacy Audit

Ei (UK) Limited
4 Doolittle Mill
Ampthill
Bedfordshire MK45 2ND
T: 01525 840090
F: 01525 840092
E: info@eiuk.com
W: www.eiuk.com

Ei (UK) provides coaching, training, teacher EQ assessment, child EQ assessment and research in the field of emotional intelligence. Their mission is to bring an understanding of emotional intelligence into home and work communities. Their web site contains a section dedicated to education. The founder of Ei (UK) wrote the book *Emotionally Intelligent Living* (Crown House Publishing, 2001). They host an annual summer conference on emotional intelligence.

Institute for Arts Therapy in Education
2–18 Britannia Row
London N1 8PA
T: 020 7704 2534
F: 020 7704 0171
E: info@arts-therapy.demon.co.uk
W: www.arts-therapy.demon.co.uk

The Institute is a fully accredited College of Higher Education, dedicated to the in-depth theoretical and practical study of artistic, imaginative and creative expression for emotional health and well-being.

Osiris Educational
63 Stixwould Road
Woodhall Spa
Lincoln LN10 6QG
T: 01526 353678
F: 01526 353063
E: enquiries@osiriseducational.co.uk
W: www.osiriseducational.co.uk

Osiris Educational offers training courses and consultancy on the application of emotional intelligence in schools. These are aimed at leaders, policy-makers and classroom practitioners.

Richmond upon Thames College
C/o Robert Owen
Egerton Road
Twickenham
Middlesex TW2 7SJ
T: 020 8607 8305/8314
F: 020 8744 9738
E: courses@richmond-utcoll.ac.uk

The College provides a series of courses around emotional literacy aimed at anyone who would like to learn more about how the concept can be applied in their work. The leadership courses are designed for anyone involved in facilitating process groups for adults or young people.

School of Emotional Literacy
Buckholdt House
The Street
Frampton-on-Severn
Gloucestershire GL2 7ED
T: 01452 741 106
F: 01452 741 520
E: info@schoolofemotional-literacy.com
W: www.schoolofemotional-literacy.com

The school provides training for a certificate in emotional literacy development that equips professionals to pass on to children and young people the life skills, attitudes, habits and values associated with emotional literacy.

Sowelu Associates
Collywell
Brownston
Nr Ivybridge
South Devon PL21 0SQ
T: 01548 82192
E: SoweluAss@aol.com
W: www. soweluassociates.co.uk
W: www.enable-online.com

Julia Bird and Lynne Gerlach integrate brain research, child development, psychology, learning theory and school effectiveness experience to offer consultancy and training on the development of emotionally competent schools. This includes the ENABLE approach (available as a CD).

Groups providing support for parents and families

Community Education Development Centre (CEDC)
Unit C1
Grovelands Court
Grovelands Estate
Longford Road Exhall
Coventry CV7 9NE
T: 024 7658 8440
F: 024 7658 8441
E: info@cedc.org.uk
W: www.cedc.org.uk

CEDC is the national charity for community-based learning. It runs a number of projects that encourage parental involvement in children's learning, including Share, Active Dads, and Parents in the Community Millennium Awards.

Family Links
New Marston Centre
1A Jack Straw's Lane
Oxford OX3 0DL
T: 01865 454004
F: 01865 452145
E: familylinksUK@aol.com
W: www.familylinks.org.uk

Family Links' Nurturing Programme provides a whole-school programme, which includes all children and school staff, and a matching programme on offer to all parents. The underlying philosophy is that one needs to be emotionally literate and healthy in order to reach one's full potential.

Parenting Education & Support Forum
Unit 431 Highgate Studios
53–79 Highgate Road
London NW5 1TL
T: 020 7284 8370
F: 020 7485 3587
E: pesf@dial.pipex.com
W: www.parenting-forum.org.uk

PESF brings together those concerned with, the education and support for parents. It promotes and maintains a high profile for parenting education and support, where education means learning in the fullest sense of growing in knowledge, skills and understanding.

Parents for Inclusion
Unit 2
70 South Lambeth Road
London SW8 1RL
T: 020 7735 7735
F: 020 7582 5008
E: info@parentsforinclusion.org
W: www.parentsforinclusion.org

Parents for Inclusion is a national charity, run by parents for parents. They have developed 'tools' for parents of disabled children by working closely with disabled adults and drawing on their understanding. The aim is to help parents become real allies to their disabled children.

School-Home Support
Unit 6, Bow Business Exchange
5 Yeo Street
London E3 3QP
T: 020 7538 3479
F: 020 7537 4361
E: mail@schoolhomesupport.org.uk
W: www.schoolhomesupport.org.uk

Provides a school-based, child-centred approach to supporting young people in school, strengthening links between schoolsand families and enabling people to work together to overcome the barriers that face children and young people.

Specialist distributors of books and resources relating to emotional literacy

BS Bookstall Forum
4a Ashbourne Road
Derby DE22 3AA
T: 01332 368039
F: 01332 368079
E: enq@bookstallforum.co.uk
W: www.bookstallforum.co.uk

Bookstall Forum is a specialist mail order supplier of books on Philosophy for Children, PSHE, child protection, social work, counselling and therapy, and working with children and young people.

Development Education Project
c/o MMU
801 Wilmslow Road
Didsbury
Manchester M20 2QR
T: 0161 445 2495
F: 0161 445 2360
E: depman@gn.apc.org
W: www.dep.org.uk/resources

DEP stocks a wide range of resources which can be used to introduce the global dimension to many areas of the curriculum including race, disability, bullying, self-esteem, citizenship, thinking skills, early years and emotional literacy. All these resources are available for sale or hire.

Incentive Plus
Unit 6 Fernfield Farm
Whaddon Road
Little Horwood
Milton Keynes MK17 0PS
T: 01908 526120
F: 01908 526130
E: info@incentiveplus.co.uk
W: www.incentiveplus.co.uk

Incentive Plus provides resources and materials for those educating for responsible participation in society. It provides materials to tackle disaffection, promote self-esteem, develop emotional literacy and address the serious issue of behaviour.

Lucky Duck Publishing
 3 Thorndale Mews
 Clifton
 Bristol BS8 2HX
 T: 0117 9732881
 F: 0117 9731707
 E: publishing@luckyduck.co.uk
 W: www.luckyduck.co.uk

Lucky Duck publishes books, videos, resources and teacher training materials on positive behaviour management. These cover topics such as self-esteem, bullying, circle time, emotional literacy, peer mediation, problem-solving, anger management and conflict resolution.

Smallwood Publishing Ltd
 The Old Bakery
 Charlton House
 Dour Street
 Dover
 Kent CT16 1ED
 T: 01304 226900 (orders)
 T: 01304 226800 (info)
 F: 01304 226700
 E: info@smallwood.co.uk
 W: www.smallwood.co.uk

Smallwood is a publisher and mail order supplier of innovative resources for mental health professionals and educators. Its subsidiary, Being Yourself, offers materials for direct work with children, including books, therapeutic games and therapists' puppets.

Words of Discovery
 Unit 33, Vulcan House
 Vulcan Road
 Leicester LE2 1SB
 T: 0116 262 2244
 F: 0116 262 2244
 E: info@wordsofdiscovery.com
 W: www.wordsofdiscovery.com

Words of Discovery aims to provide the best possible collection of books from around the world to promote children's beliefs, values, self-esteem, creativity, communication, personal and social awareness.

Networks and groups for young people's emotional well-being and learning

Article 31 Action Network
Play Train
The Post Office Buildings
149–153 Alcester Road
Mosely
Birmingham B13 8JW
T: 0121 449 6665
F: 0121 449 8221
E: team@playtrain.org.uk
W: www.playtrain.org.uk

The Article 31 Children's Consultancy Scheme enables children to act as specialist consultants to arts, media and leisure service providers. It improves the quality of services to children and families and, at the same time, helps to implement the United Nations Convention on the rights of the child, by enabling children's views to be taken into account in decisions that directly affect them.

Curiosity & Imagination
Kids' Clubs Network
Bellerive House
3 Muirfield Crescent
London E14 9SZ
T: 020 7522 6919
F: 020 7512 2010
E: info@curiosityandimagination.org.uk
W: www.curiosityandimagination.org.uk

A UK-wide network dedicated to inspiring children's exploration of the world around them through hands-on activities in a whole range of settings including schools, libraries, out-of-school clubs, childcare facilities, youth clubs, historical sites, museums and designated Centres for Curiosity and Imagination.

Emotional Health Alliance for Children
C/o The National Pyramid Trust
84 Uxbridge Road
London W13 8RA
T: 020 8579 5108
F: 020 8579 5108
E: EHA@chanceuk.com

The EHA is made up of organisations working to help children with social and emotional issues to flourish at school and at home. EHA believe that the most effective early intervention works in a gentle, non-stigmatising and low-key way.

The National Mentoring Network
First Floor Charles House
Albert Street
Eccles M30 0PW
T: 0161 787 8600
W: 0161 787 8100
E: enquiries@nmn.org.uk
W: www.nmn.org.uk

A membership-based organisation that supports the growth of mentoring in its various forms. Its aims are to promote the development of mentoring; offer advice and support to those wishing to set up or develop mentoring programmes and to provide a forum for the exchange of information and good practice.

The Nurture Group Network
24 Murray Mews
London NW1 9RJ
T: 020 7485 2025
F: 020 7485 2025
E: info@nurturegroups.org
W: www.nurturegroups.org

The Nurture Group Network supports school improvement by promoting emotional development and improvements in behaviour. They also achieve improved attainments, better attendance, greater parental involvement, and improved home relationships by working directly with schools and LEAs.

Useful web-based resources

CASEL (The Collaborative for Academic, Social and Emotional Learning)
www.casel.org

CASEL collaborates with an international network of leading researchers and practitioners in the fields of social and emotional learning, positive youth development, character education and school reform.

Centre for Social and Emotional Education (CSEE)
www.csee.net

Provides parents, educators and mental health professionals with resources that promote social and emotional skills and knowledge in children and adolescents.

Committee for Children
www.cfchildren.org

Developer of programmes for social and emotional learning, including the violence prevention curriculum Second Steps.

Educationalists
www.educationalists.co.uk

Online resource providing articles, case studies, reports, features, conferences and seminars to support school-based, further, higher and lifelong learning.

Emotional Literacy Advocates
www.nwlink.com/~emolit/

A non-profit community service that promotes better communication by building awareness of the relationship between language and emotions through the arts.

Emotional Literacy Education and Self-Knowledge
www.emotionalliteracyeducation.com

A general site on all aspects of emotional literacy, self-education and how to make the world a better place.

EQ Network Europe
http://www.eqeurope.6seconds.org/

Provides a network for trainers, teachers and counsellors who are interested in emotional intelligence within their work or profession.

International Council for Self-Esteem
http://www.self-esteem-international.org

Promotes public and personal awareness of the benefits of a healthy sense of self-esteem and personal responsibility.

Kids EQ: The Children's Emotional Literacy Project
www.kidseq.com

Set up by the Foundation for the Education of Emotional Literacy (FEEL) to educate professionals and lay people about thenature of feelings as a source of human energy, information and influence.

The National Emotional Literacy Interest Group
www.nelig.com

Launched in 2000 as a web site through which initiatives and good practice in emotional literacy – across the UK and beyond – could be disseminated.

Pupiline
www.pupiline.net

A web site written, designed, edited and managed by young people for young people. Pupiline has grown to cover all kinds of issues that affect young people including bullying, friends and family, exam stress, school, dating, health, part-time jobs and many other topics.

School Emotional Health Education Project
www.emotionalhonesty.com

Ronald Brill published *Emotional Honesty & Self-Acceptance: Education Strategies for Preventing Violence* in 2000, and has gone on to develop *Lizards: The Feeling Game* to help students prevent harmful acts. 'Games like this,' he says, 'help students accept both themselves and their feelings, since they de-stigmatise feeling hurt' as a result of loss, rejection, betrayal and humiliation.

Six Seconds
www.6seconds.org

Organisation dedicated to improving relationships by teaching EQ in schools, organisations, and communities around the globe. It provides consultancy and training, as well as publishing materials around its Self Science curriculum.

Claude Steiner
www.claudesteiner.com

Provides information on the importance of emotions and the effect they have in our lives and in our personal power.

Teachernet
www.teachernet.gov.uk/pshe

Set up by the DfES for teachers of Personal, Social and Health Education (PSHE) and Citizenship, the site supports all aspects of PSHE.

Transforming Conflict
www.transformconflict.org/

An informative web site which provides materials and approaches to citizenship and human rights education and support for partnership work with other schools in a cross-community, cross-border and transnational context.

Transforming Schools
www.transformingschools.org.uk

A web portal designed to offer a simple and effective way through the vast quantity of information on innovation in schools and learning.

References

Aulls, M. (1998) 'Contributions to classroom discourses to what content students learn during curriculum enactment'. *Journal of Educational Psychology*, 90(1).

Barlow, J. and Stewart-Brown, S.L. (2001) 'Understanding parenting programmes: parents' views'. *Primary Health Care and Research and Development*, 2, 117–30.

Bausch, L. (2001) 'The story of their lives: understanding our students' literacy practices and events'. *Networks: An On-line Journal for Teacher Research*, 4(2).

Channon, H. (2000) *Evaluation Report for Cumbria County Council Psychological Services* (unpublished).

Claxton, G. (1999) *Wise Up: The Challenge of Lifelong Learning*. London: Bloomsbury.

Claxton, G. (2003) *Building Learning Power*. Bristol: TLO.

Damasio, A.R. (1996) *Descartes' Error: Emotion, Reason and the Human Brain*. London: Papermac.

Damasio, A.R. (2000) *The Feeling of What Happens: Body and Emotion in the Making of Consciousness*. London: William Heinemann.

Deakin-Crick, R., Broadfoot, P. and Claxton G. (2002) *Developing an Effective Lifelong Learning Inventory* (unpublished).

Donoahue, Z. (1998) 'Giving children control: fourth graders initiate and sustain discussions after teacher read-alouds'. *Networks: An On-Line Journal for Teacher Research*, 1(1).

Fielding, M. (2001a), 'Young people as researchers', in *The Antidote Real Dialogue Conference Brochure*, May.

Fielding, M. (2001b) 'Beyond the rhetoric of student voice: new departures or new constraints in the transformation of 21st century schooling'. *Forum*, 43(2) 100–10.

Hall, E. and Kirkland, A. (1984) 'Drawing of trees and the expression of feelings in early adolescence'. *British Journal of Guidance and Counselling*, 12(1).

Hanko, G. (1999) *Increasing Competence through Collaborative Problem-Solving: Using Insight into Social and Emotional Factors in Children's Learning*. London: David Fulton.

Hannam, D. (2001) 'Attitudes, attainment, attendance and exclusion in secondary schools that take student participation seriously'. Paper presented to ESRC seminar Pupil Voice and Democracy, 15 October.

Hansen, L. (2001) 'The inherent desire to learn: intrinsically motivating first grade students'. *Networks: An On-line Journal for Teacher Research*, 4(2).

Harding, C. (2001) 'Students as researchers is as important as the National Curriculum'. *Forum*, 43(2), 56–7.

Hay McBer (2000) *Research into Teacher Effectiveness: A model of teacher effectiveness*. Report to the Department for Education and Employment, June.

REFERENCES

Hope, P. and Sharland, P. (1997) *Tomorrow's Parents: Developing Parenting Education in Schools*. London: The Calouste Gulbenkian Foundation.

Hunt, H. and Crow, G. (2001) *'Taking Care': A Whole School Emotional Literacy Project*. Evaluation summary and strategic questions (unpublished).

Izard, C., Fine, S.S., Schultz, D. *et al.* (2001) 'Emotional knowledge as a predictor of social behaviour and academic competence in children at risk'. *Psychological Science*, **12** 18–23.

Johnson, D.W. and Johnson, R. T. (1994) *Learning Together and Alone: Cooperative, Competitive and Individualistic Learning (4th Edition)*, US Imports and PHIPEs.

Layton, M. (1996) *An Evaluation of the Effectiveness of the School and Family Links Programme*, as part of an MA dissertation, Oxford Brookes University, School of Education (unpublished).

LeDoux, J. (1998) *The Emotional Brain: The Mysterious Underpinnings of Emotional Life*. London: Weidenfeld & Nicolson.

McCallum, B., Hargreaves, E. and Gipps, C. (2000) 'Learning: The Pupil's Voice'. *Cambridge Journal of Education*, **30**(2).

McCombs, B. and Whisler, J.S. (1998) *The Learner-centered Classroom and School*. San Francisco: Jossey-Bass.

Mathews, B. (2001) 'Dialogue and Science Education' in: *Antidote's Real Dialogue Conference Brochure*, March.

Moss, H. and Wilson, V. (1998) 'Using Circle Time in a Primary School'. *Pastoral Care*, September.

Nias, J. (1996) 'Thinking About Feeling: the emotions in teaching'. *Cambridge Journal of Education*, **26**(3), 293–306.

Osler, A. (1998) 'Children's rights, responsibilities and understandings of school discipline'. *Research Papers in Education*, **15**, 49–67.

Robinson, W.P. and Tayler, C.A. (1999) 'An evaluation of a circle time programme for Year 7 pupils', University of Bristol (unpublished report).

Seigle, P., cited in *Caring Classrooms/Intelligent Schools: The Social and Emotional Education of Young Children*, J. Cohen (ed.) (2001) 108–20. New York and London: Teachers College Press, Columbia University.

Sharp, P. and Faupel, A. (eds) (2002) *Promoting Emotional Literacy: Guidelines for Schools, Local Authorities, and the Health Services*. Southampton Emotional Literacy Group, Southampton City Council Local Education Authority. Can be obtained from www.nelig.com/eligs-selig.html.

West, M. and Patterson, M. (1999) 'The Workforce and Productivity'. *New Economy*. **6**(1), March.

Wheatcroft School (2001) 'Working as a Team: Children and teachers learning from each other'. *Forum*, **43**(2), 51–3.

Winstanley, C. (2001) 'Student Teachers Exploring P4C', *Antidote's Real Dialogue Conference Brochure*, May.

Witherow, A. (1998) 'Case Study 2 Jack Lobley School'. *Quality Circle Time, The Heart of the Curriculum*, Conference Brochure produced by Antidote and the Self-Esteem Network.

Index